SANTA FE ART

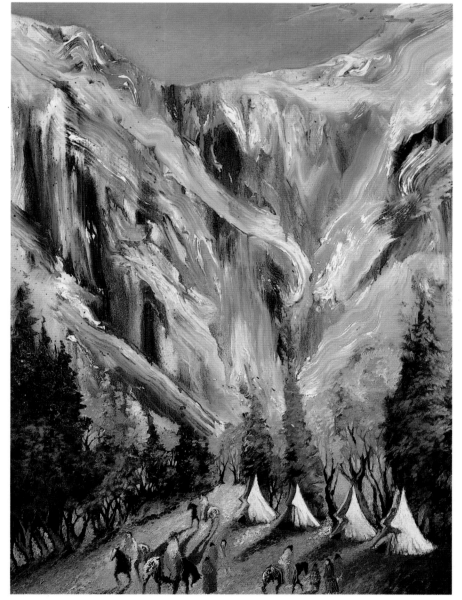

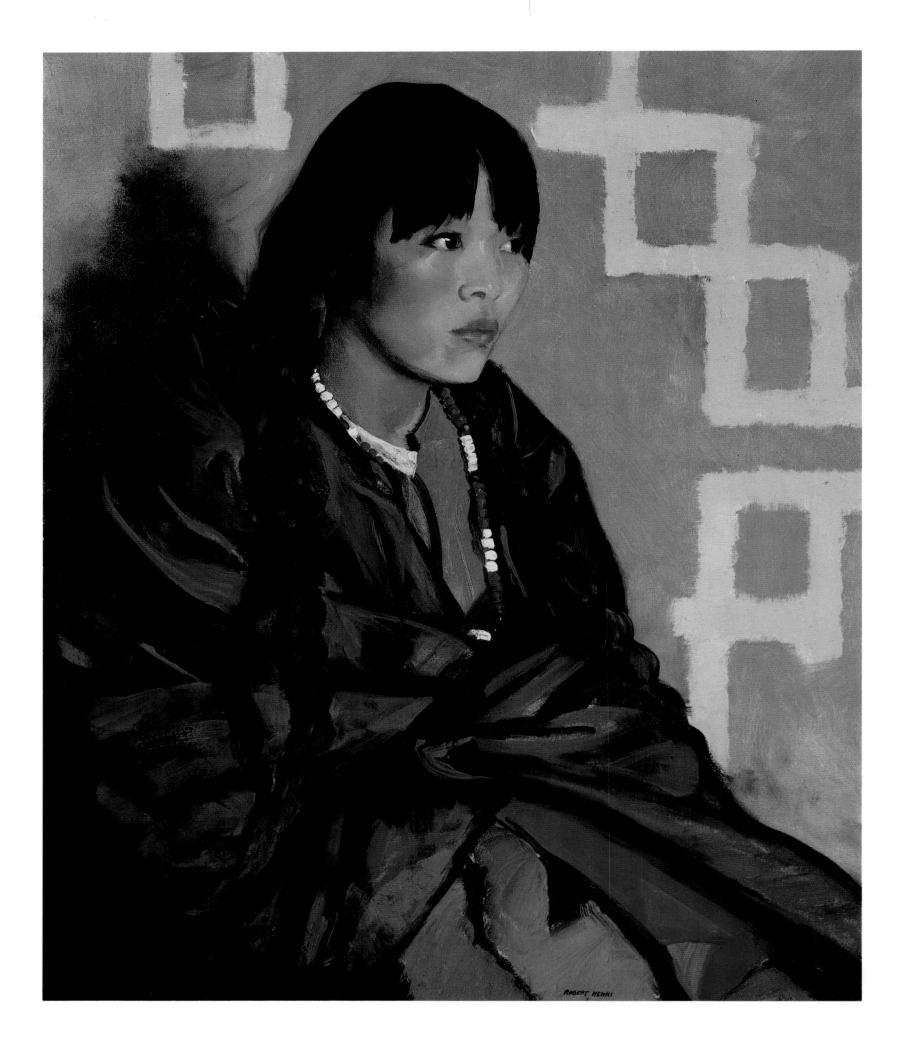

SANTA FE ART

Simone Ellis

JG PRESS

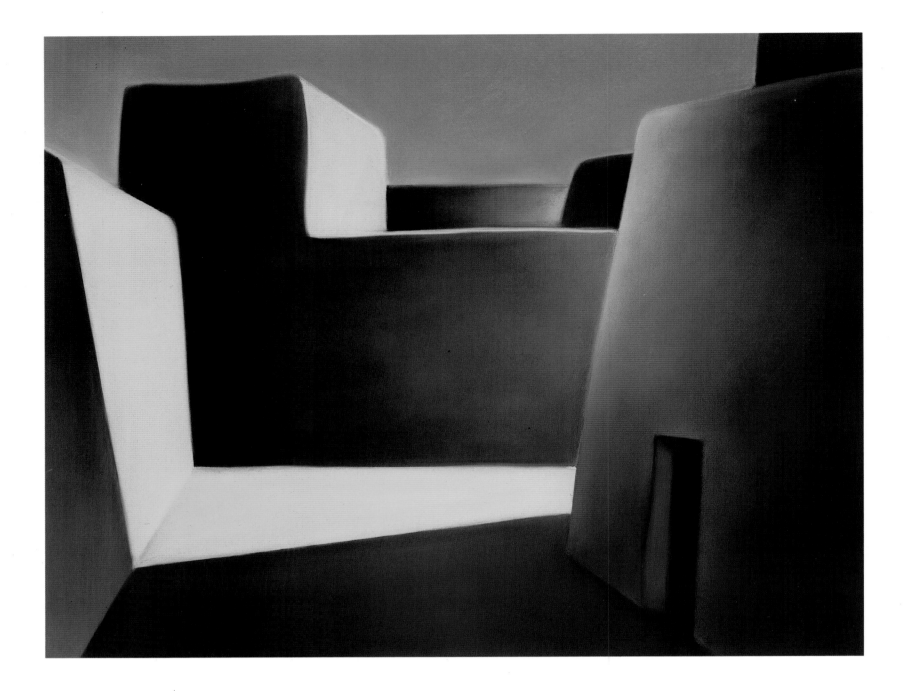

Page 1:
EARL BISS
Home Again in the Shelter of the Beartooth Range
1992, oil on canvas, 40 × 30 in.
Collection of the Artist
Photo courtesy Joyner Publications Ltd.

Page 2:
ROBERT HENRI
Indian Girl (Julianita)
1917, oil on canvas, 32 × 26 in.
© *1992 Indianapolis Museum of Art, IN*

Above:
MARGARET NES
Lightshaft and Walls
1990, pastel on paper, 20¾ × 26¼ in.
Collection of Robert Kuncio and Sarah Raleigh
Photo courtesy of the Edith Lambert Gallery, Santa Fe, NM

Dedicated to the memory of Sara Ellis and Giannina Passalacqua.

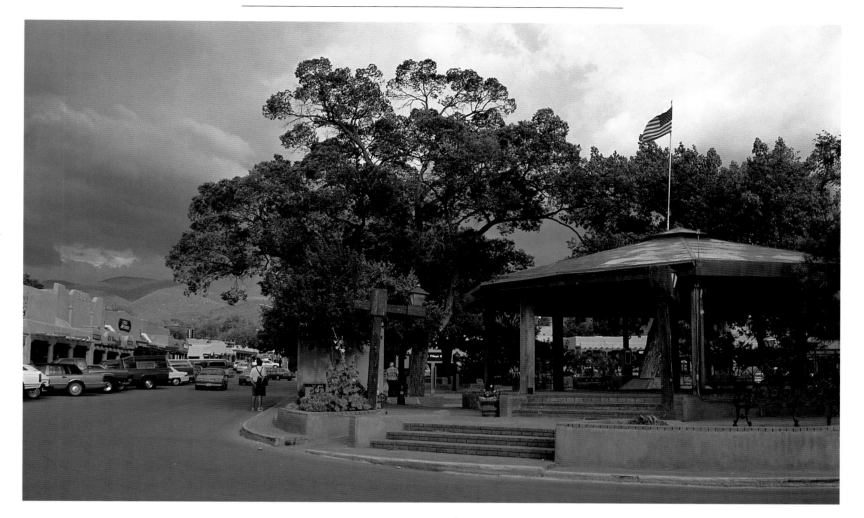

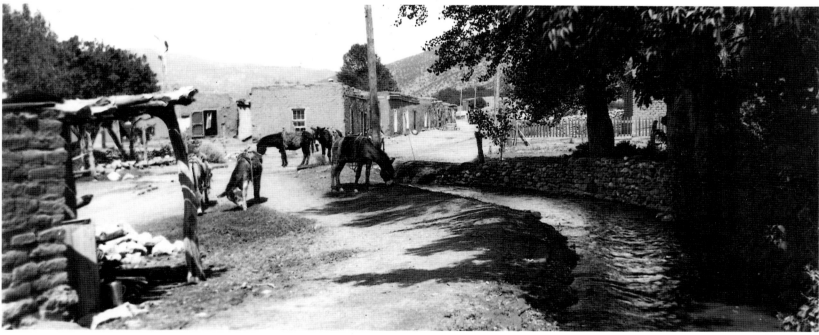

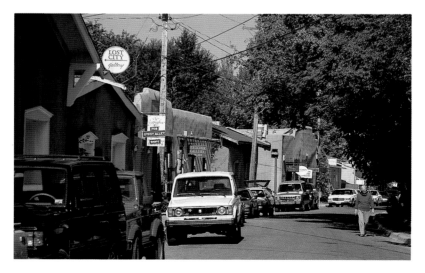

Top left and right: Taos Plaza in 1880 and 1992.
Above: Canyon Road at Acequia Madre in Santa Fe, ca. 1915. At the time, Canyon Road served as a burro trail to the piñon-studded hills for firewood.
Left: A modern-day view up Canyon Road, the heart of Santa Fe's art colony.
Page 8, top: A photo taken by Bert Geer Phillips of Ernest Blumenschein with the broken wagon that caused the first art colony to be established at Taos, 1898.
Page 8, bottom: Catharine C. Critcher, the only female member of the Taos Society of Artists, in her studio.

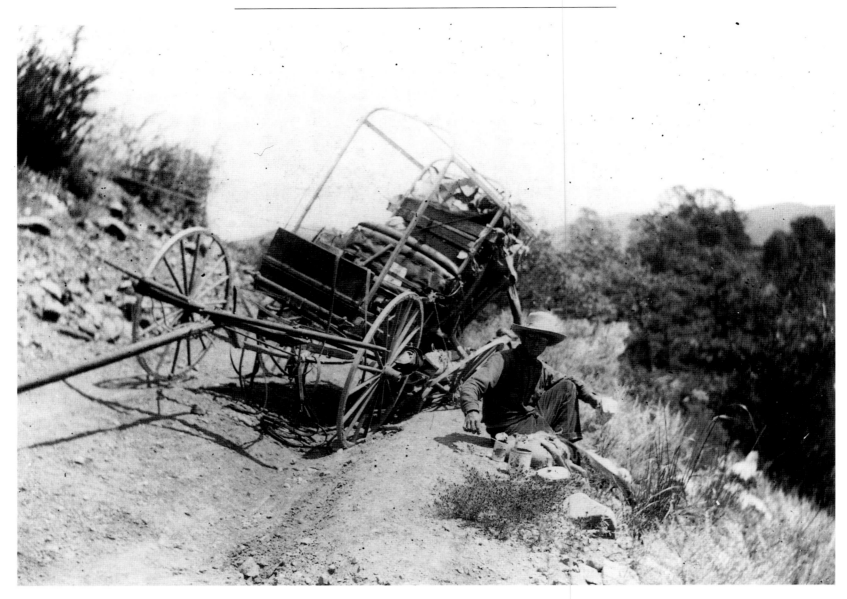

the Spanish. The Spanish villages that the newly arriving artists found had been there for 300 years, or nearly 100 years longer than the United States has been in existence.

The Anglo artists were essentially the first of the Euro-Americans to settle in the Southwestern villages of Taos and Santa Fe. They were illustrators on assignment, trainees fresh from the École des Beaux-Arts and L'Académie Julian in Paris. They were survivors of WWI gas attacks, or victims of tuberculosis in search of a more healthy climate. They were painters, sculptors and printmakers who were seeking new material. They were the Gauguins of the American Southwest, in a land as exotic and isolated as Tahiti, filled with sights that bewildered the eyes of first-time visitors, and beckoned them back again and again to interpret what they saw. They were women and men, young and aging, mostly from the East Coast and some from the West, such as Fremont Ellis who came from El Paso, Texas. Some were émigrés, such as Leon Gaspard, who was born in Vitebsk, Russia.

The first established group of exhibiting artists in the Southwest was the Taos Society of Artists (1915-27). Founded by Bert Phillips, W. Herbert Dunton, Joseph Sharp, Oscar Berninghaus, E. I. Couse and Ernest Blumenschein, the group expanded over the years to include E. Martin Hennings, Walter Ufer, Kenneth Adams, Victor Higgins and Catharine Critcher. Critcher, at the time a well-known painter who had

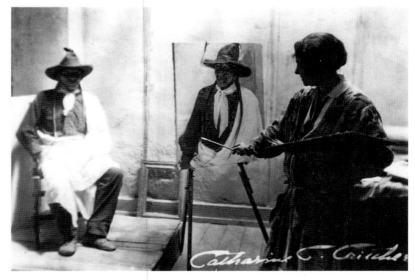

studied in Paris, is the only artist of the eleven whose work has fallen into obscurity. There were numerous women painters in the early colonies, including Mary Greene Blumenschein (Ernest's wife), whose work suffered the same fate. But considering that it wasn't until 1920 that women were granted the right to vote, the fact that women's paintings were not considered as important as the men's is not surprising. In fact, it is astonishing that so many young women "of family" made their way to the "dangerous" Wild West to paint.

In the summer of 1919 Randall Davey and John Sloan, members of the Ashcan School of painting, decided to take a road

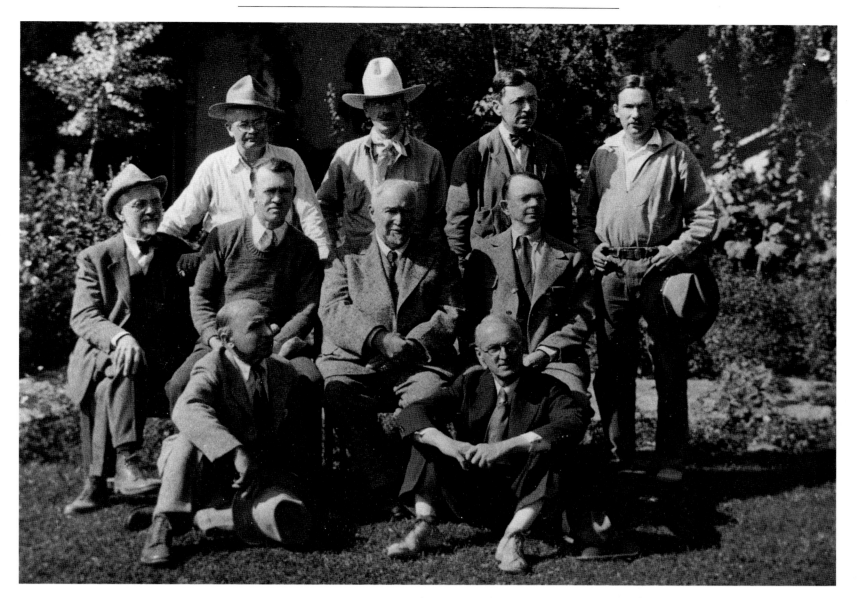

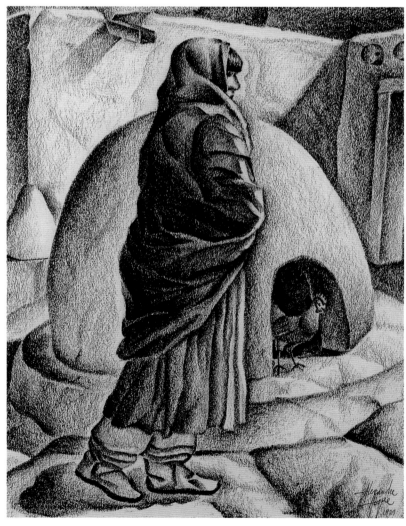

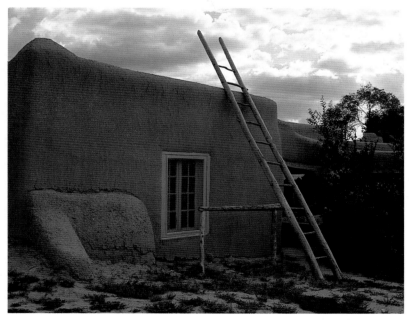

Top: The ten male members of the Taos Society of Artists, in 1927: (top, l-r) Walter Ufer, W. Herbert Dunton, Victor Higgins, Kenneth Adams; (middle, l-r): Joseph Sharp, E. Martin Hennings, E.I. Couse, Oscar Berninghaus; (bottom, l-r): Bert Phillips, Ernest Blumenschein.
Left: Alexandre Hogue (1898 –   ), *Taos Pueblo Woman*, 1929, lithocrayon on paper, 11¼ × 8 in., Cline Fine Art Gallery, Santa Fe, NM. Now 94 and still working, Hogue was a long-time friend of the early Taos painters.
Above: The Blumenschein House, on Ledoux Street in Taos.

trip out West with their wives. They had heard about the isolated communities in New Mexico from their mentor, Robert Henri, and as Sloan recalled on a radio show hosted by Alfred Morang, "The next thing I knew I was involved in the purchase of an old 1912 chaindriven Simplex racing car, setting out for Santa Fe, which Henri had recommended as the best climate in the world." Both Davey and Sloan continued to return to New Mexico for the summer painting season, eventually settling in Santa Fe permanently.

By the time many of the early Taos and Santa Fe artists arrived, they already held firmly established reputations as illustrators for such publications as *Scribner's*, *Harper's* and *McClure's*. They illustrated stories by the greatest writers of the day, such as Jack London and Rudyard Kipling. They were realistic renderers by training and trade, but many had been exposed to the color theories of the European Impressionists, Post-Impressionists, Pointillists, Cubists and Fauvists, via the Parisian schools. The works of Gauguin, Cézanne and van Gogh were familiar, very early on, to the pioneer Southwestern painters. Among others, Gustave Moreau was on the faculty at the École des Beaux-Arts while the Southwestern painters studied there. Moreau was an influential teacher to Matisse, Rouault and Derain, among other European Fauvist painters.

The American painters also shared a passion with the Europeans for Japanese woodblock prints found in boxes of china shipped to Europe, after the trade barrier from the Far East was dropped in 1854. Blumenschein's home in Taos, which is now a museum, features one entire room filled with Japanese woodblock prints.

The early Southwestern painters combined the frontal composition of the Japanese artists and the radical color theories of the turn of the century European painters with the imagery of the New Mexican desert landscapes and Pueblo dances to create a vibrant new form of American art.

The new European and American painters shocked the world with their non-realistic, frontal paintings, utilizing wild color schemes, such as orange pathways and purple haystacks. A huge show of nearly 2000 works of art was displayed for the first time in America at the 1913 Armory Show in New York. Included in the show were works by John Sloan, Robert Henri, Marsden Hartley, John Marin and Andrew Dasburg, all of whom would work in the Southwest.

The Armory Show was the accepted turning point for American art. The radical new work shown there met with both critical disdain and wild enthusiasm, but what is more important than the reception was the permission the show con-

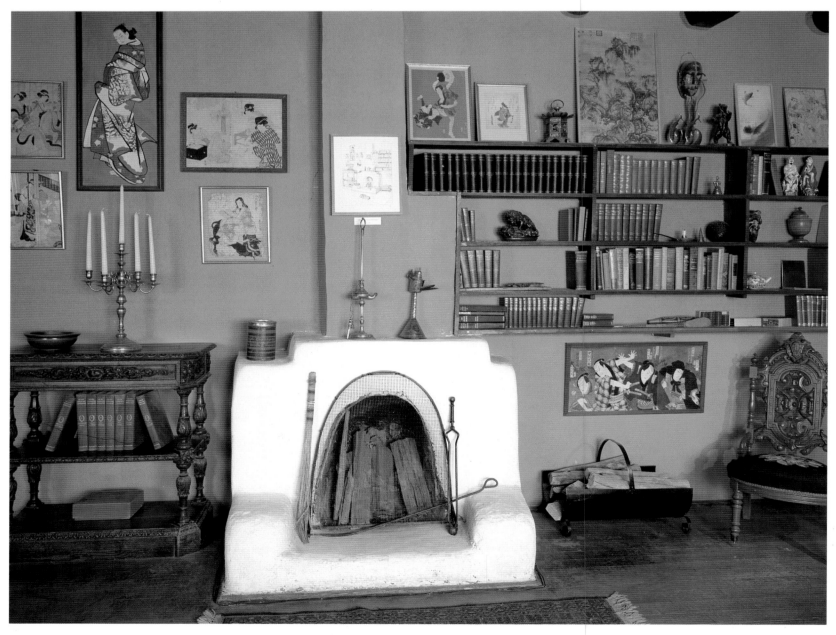

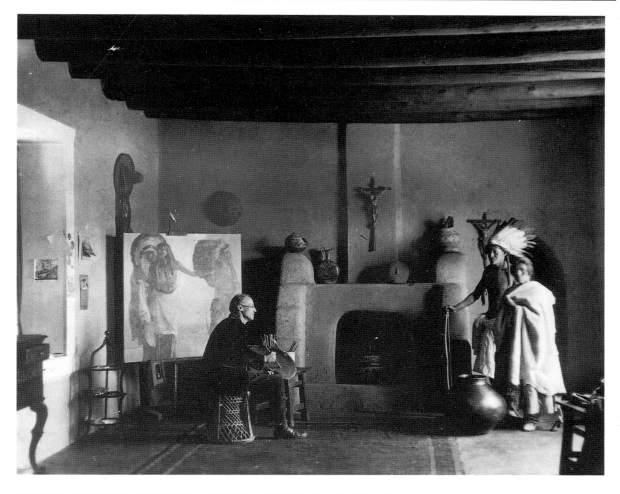

Page 10: Japanese woodblock prints, which influenced the early Taos artists, hang in this room in the Blumenschein House. Other rooms contain nineteenth-century Native American paintings, African masks, works by the members of the Taos Society of Artists, and works by Mary Greene Blumenschein. The Blumenschein House is a National Historic Landmark owned by the Kit Carson Memorial Foundation.
Left: Ernest Blumenschein in his studio, 1926.
Below left: (l-r) Marsden Hartley, Randall Davey, and John Sloan at the Palace of the Governors in Santa Fe, September 1919.
Bottom left: The Randall Davey House, at the top of Canyon Road in Santa Fe, is now part of the Audubon Society.

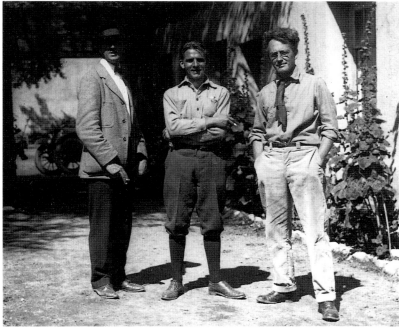

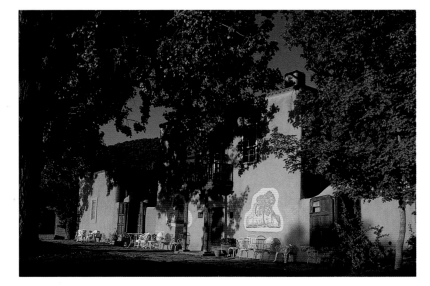

ferred on artists to paint freely and to explore new ideas and ways of seeing.

Once in the Southwest, these illustrators by trade ripped off their academic shrouds and began to paint. Realistic painters depicting surrealistic scenes, they documented the ritual dances (which have changed very little to this day) through the eyes of the participants, their vision inevitably altered by the experience of the ritual they were painting. They immersed themselves in the magical changing light of the desert-scapes before them, and found the Fauvist lavender to actually exist in the lining of a billowing, motionless cloud. A pathway really was orange, and the dancing Pueblo people were truly wearing deer horns and rabbit skins on their heads, as they danced in perfect unison with 300 villagers.

While the realists were hard at work, in 1921 five young painters in Santa Fe who defined themselves as "Modernists" formed a group for the purpose of exhibitions, and named themselves Los Cinco Pintores. These artists – Józef Bakoś, Walter Mruk, Willard Nash, Will Shuster and Fremont Ellis – all were under the age of 30 at the time, and most of them spent the rest of their lives in the Southwest.

As opposed to the objective or realistic painters who had arrived before them, the Modernists held that twentieth-century painting was about looking inward and drawing metaphors about personal freedom from the outer world around them. Though in opposition to Sloan, Davey, Blumenschein and the other representational painters in ideology, Los Cinco Pintores were also known to cross over. In fact, founding member Józef Bakoś also belonged to a broader-based group of painters founded two years after Los Cinco Pintores in 1923,

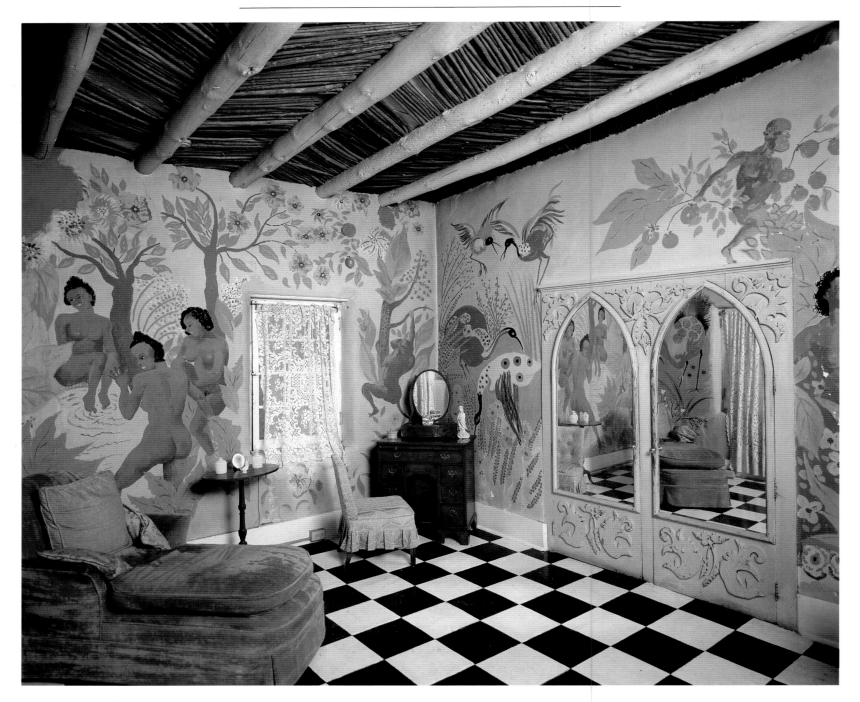

simply called the New Mexico Painters. This group included talents such as Blumenschein, Ufer, Sloan, Dasburg and Frank Applegate in their exhibitions.

With the arrival of the young Modernists in New Mexico, the three styles of painting that co-exist in Santa Fe to this day were established: Landscape (including abstracted landscapes), Figurative (including the Pueblo dance genre paintings) and Abstract Modernist.

As John Sloan pointed out in the 1920s, one of the reasons that he returned every summer to paint in Santa Fe was that he could paint in any style that he wanted to, and that there was no dogmatic party-line to dictate *how* one was supposed to paint.

This freedom still exists in today's contemporary market. One can see it clearly by looking at galleries such as the Munson Gallery on Canyon Road, which presents abstract works by such veterans of the medium as William Lumpkins side by side with the soft realism of Elias Rivera. In the Cline Gallery, also on Canyon Road, one can find abstract Emil Bisttrams hanging next to contemporary realist genre paintings

by Eli Levin. The Gerald Peters Gallery shows work from the earliest representatives of all three styles – Gaspard, to Applegate, to Bakoś and O'Keeffe – hanging next to contemporary works by visionary figurative painters such as Douglas Johnson.

As for the success of the different schools of thought, the collecting public has tended to support all three styles of painting. The painters themselves, though in opposition on the canvas, also always have socialized together, and avoided stances that excluded others strictly on ideological principles. In fact, the Southwest is one of the few places in America where artists of all walks of life, culture and ideology paint side by side, year in and year out, exploring the same visual stimuli, and coming up with vastly different interpretations.

In fact, the earliest "wall art" to exist in this area, the petroglyphs of the Anasazi (the "old ones", or ancestors of the current Pueblo peoples according to oral legend), included both representational and symbolic abstract images. This ideological symbiosis could be explained away by the isolation of the area, but more likely it springs from intrinsic qualities in the high deserts of New Mexico.

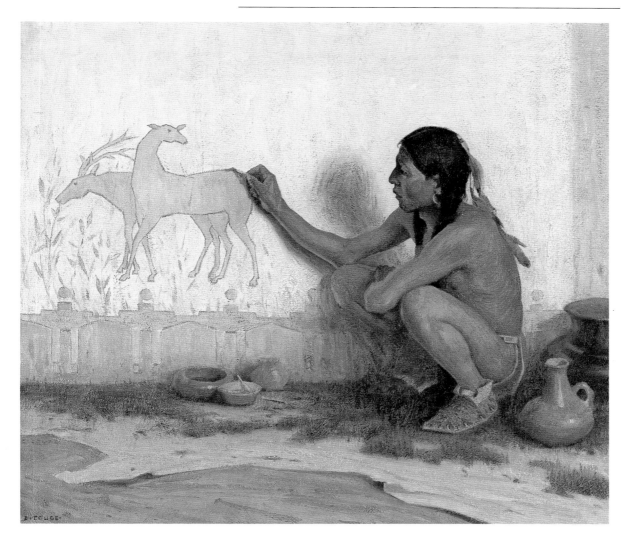

Page 12: The dressing room in the Randall Davey House is decorated with frescoes of dark-skinned women reminiscent of Gauguin's. Note the cross-hatched ceiling.
Left: Eanger Irving Couse, *Indian Artist*, 1920, oil on canvas, 24 × 29 in., Collection of Virginia Couse Levitt, Photo by Addison Doty. Couse's portrait of a young Indian meticulously painting a portrait of a deer on a cave wall shows Couse's heightened sensitivity to the origins of painting in the Southwest.
Below left: Walter Chappell's photograph of Chaco Canyon pictographs demonstrates that abstraction is an age-old art in the Southwest.
Below: Compare the lines in these Navajo sand paintings to the lines in Emil Bisttram's painting *The Voices of Silence* (page 16).

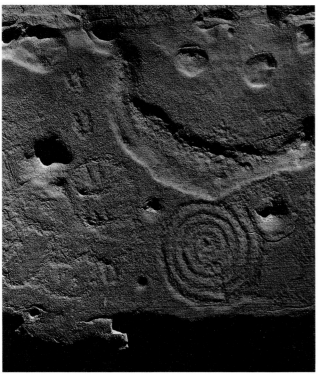

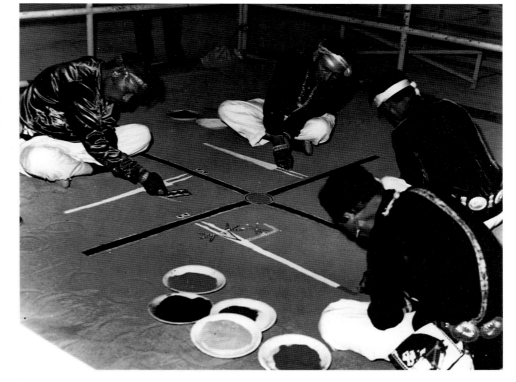

As Marsden Hartley put it in a letter written to Alfred Stieglitz in October of 1919, from Taos, where he came as a guest of Mabel Dodge Luhan (the Gertrude Stein of the Southwest, who was responsible for bringing the great majority of the early painters to New Mexico): "My work has the abstraction underneath it all now & that is what I was working toward & what I deliberately set out to do down here, for this is the perfect realistic abstraction in landscape."

As with the illustrators-turned-painters, Hartley was com-

pletely taken with the color, light and shapes of the desert: ". . . great isolated altar-like forms . . . stand alone on a great mesa with immensities of blue around them and that strange Indian red earth making almost unearthly foregrounds." (Letter to Stieglitz, June 24, 1918).

In 1929, as the rest of America's art centers hit rock bottom, the Santa Fe and Taos colonies hit their peak. By that time, there were an estimated 250 artists in Santa Fe. The Taos colony had also grown, but not nearly as fast as Santa Fe, probably because of its more difficult accessibility.

One of the artists who arrived in New Mexico in 1929 was Georgia O'Keeffe. O'Keeffe, who was married to New York photographer Alfred Stieglitz (who nearly singlehandedly made photography the art form it is today), went to New Mexico with Rebecca Salsbury James, the wife of photographer Paul Strand. Stieglitz was a mover and shaker in the New York art world, and a close friend of many of the early artists who migrated to the Southwest. Both Stieglitz and O'Keeffe were friends of Mabel Dodge Luhan, who invited the ladies out for the summer of 1929.

It was that summer that O'Keeffe painted one of her most famous images: *Black Cross, New Mexico.* Though she had painted desert abstractions before (in Canyon, Texas, where she taught school), *Black Cross* was one of her most powerful works to date. As evidence of how little things have changed in the region, the cross that O'Keeffe painted still stands on the same spot, behind the Mabel Dodge Luhan House on the edge of Taos Pueblo land.

Few people, whether generally interested in art or not, aren't familiar with the sensuous poppies, mysterious landscapes, and graceful, illusory architectural paintings by Georgia O'Keeffe. Perhaps this is simply because these works are completely original and universally appealing, although partially also due to the fact that her husband wielded hefty power in New York and was promoting her. Therefore, unlike many of the other early women painters, O'Keeffe's beautiful, imaginative paintings and pastels are available today for public viewing, in museum collections and in books.

But, as this book demonstrates, O'Keeffe was not experimenting visually in the total isolation that many imagine. It was not a matter of lightning suddenly striking this remarkable painter, but more a matter of a combination of circumstances, including the rich, experimentally free environment of artists that she joined in 1929, the light and shapes of her surroundings, and the spirit and antiquity of the area. O'Keeffe's evolutionary leap in painting was a natural outcome of the northern New Mexican desert colonies.

The fact that the Great Depression altered Santa Fe and Taos very little was due to the fact that the New Mexico colonies were already geared toward subsistence living – a way of being on the land that dates back tens of thousands of years, and is fundamentally still the modus operandi of the art colonies in Santa Fe and Taos in the late twentieth century.

With few exceptions to the rule, such as the independently wealthy or the very famous and internationally collected who enjoy the material benefits of the Southwest's mansions and grand desert estates, the majority of Santa Fe and Taos artists live from show to show and hand to mouth, much as they did in the early days. Like the early painters, they manage to create studio spaces to paint in (always geared towards the light, of course), and they go out on the Friday Gallery Crawl to see what their contemporaries are doing, just like artists did years ago, only then they would go from studio to studio instead.

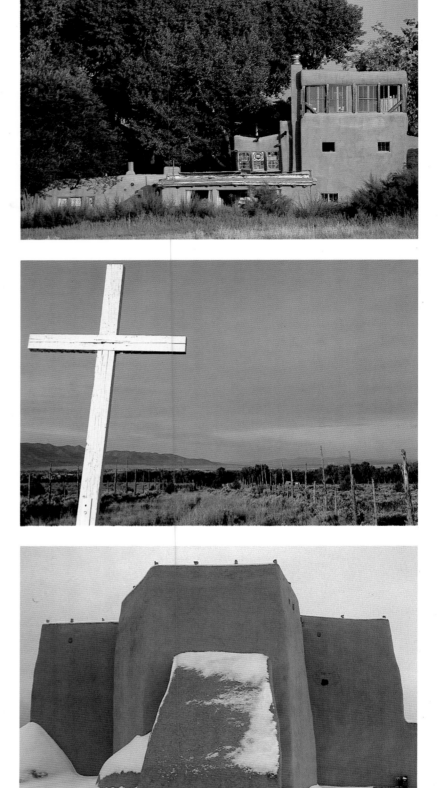

And somehow, on a wing and a prayer, they stay alive to keep painting.

As contemporary artist Mark Spencer said when asked about why so many different kinds of artists live in harmony in the same place: "Artists live on faith, and Santa Fe means the City of Holy Faith."

Another fundamentally important painter who arrived for a three-month visit in New Mexico in 1929 and who would go even farther into the visual world of abstraction than O'Keeffe did, was the Transcendentalist, Emil Bisttram.

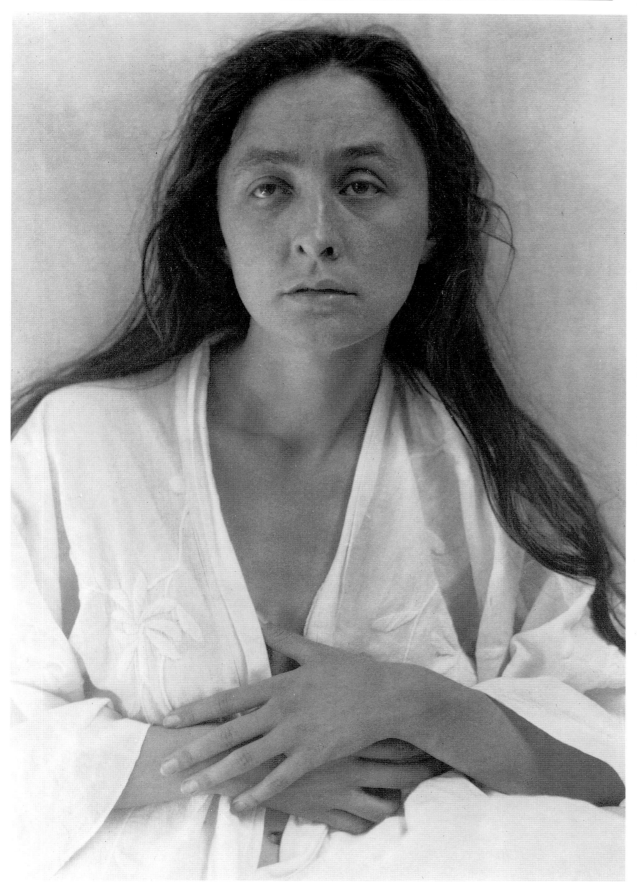

Page 14, top: The Mabel Dodge Luhan House in Taos. The wealthy Mabel Dodge (she later married Tony Luhan, a Taos Indian) arrived in Taos from New York in December 1917, and was instrumental in bringing many artists to the Southwest as her guests. Georgia O'Keeffe arrived there in 1929, and spent her summers in Taos until 1949, when she settled in Abiquiu.

Page 14, center: The Penitente cross that served as the subject for Georgia O'Keeffe's 1929 painting *Black Cross, New Mexico* (see page 64) still stands on Taos Pueblo land behind the Mabel Dodge Luhan House.

Page 14, bottom: Lisa Law's photograph of the back of the Ranchos de Taos church in winter. The picturesque church was the subject of numerous works by Georgia O'Keeffe and other artists.

Left: This photograph of Georgia O'Keeffe was taken by Alfred Stieglitz in 1918.

Bisttram was born in Europe on the Hungarian-Rumanian border 100 miles south of Budapest in 1895. He grew up as an imigrant in New York's Irish Buggy Row and became a boxer, though he was determined to become an artist.

Bisttram studied with many great teachers in New York in the early 1900s, and acquired a passion for Dynamic Symmetry, a methodology of proportion used by the ancient Egyptians and Greeks for building temples. This system utilizes lines drawn across the picture plane that allow the artist to balance the composition with a precise sense of weight, mass and volume.

It was the Dynamic Symmetry system, as well as techniques he learned from Mexican muralist Diego Rivera, with whom he interned in Mexico in 1931, that Bisttram brought to the Southwest.

By the time he moved to Taos in 1932, where he and his wife, Mayrion, rented a guest house from E. I. Couse, one of the legendary early arrivals, Bisttram was well on his way to developing an ideology that proposed that the creation of a work of art is capable of transforming the artist who creates it. This radical new point of view was called Transcendentalism.

Emil Bisttram in Taos and a recent arrival in Santa Fe, Raymond Jonson, bridged the canyon between the two colonies and founded the Transcendentalist School in 1938. It included a membership that was not recorded in the same scholarly fashion as the earlier Taos Society of Artists had been, and therefore is much more mysterious historically. The Transcendentalists embraced a vast scope of styles and expression. Both Bisttram and Jonson were strong advocates of abstraction, but Alfred Morang, who wrote their manifesto, was a representational painter.

Morang was the van Gogh of the Southwest. He painted in surrealistic, thickly applied layers, on sized workshirts and masonite board. His wiggly lines created genre paintings of bar scenes on Canyon Road, as compared to the vaporous blue abstractions by Jonson, and the bold, mystical symbolic paintings by Bisttram.

A very young Beatrice Mandelman was the anomaly of the group, with her fascinating abstract primaries, black and white Cubist compositions. William Lumpkins also joined the group,

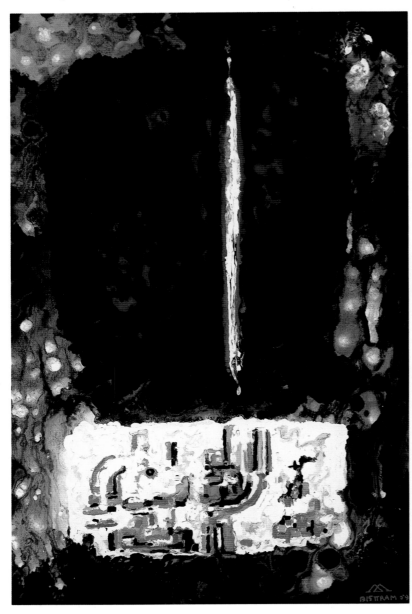

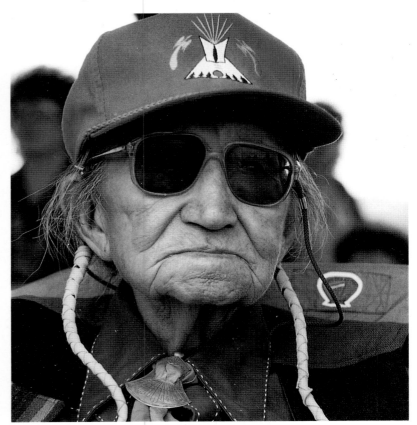

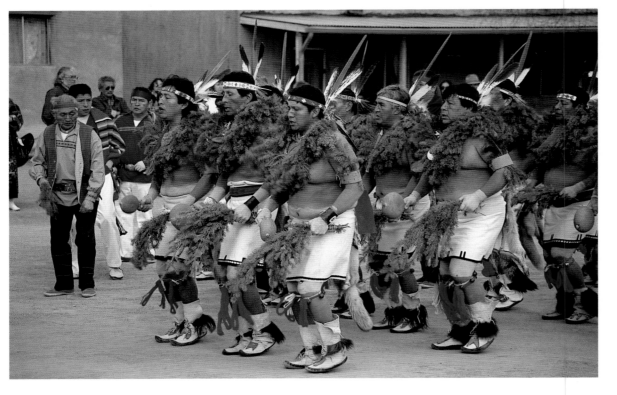

Above left: Emil Bisttram, *The Voices of Silence*, 1959, oil on panel, 40 × 27 in., Mission Gallery, Taos, NM.
Above: This photograph of Telesfor Good Morning, an elder of the Taos Pueblo, was taken in 1992. He bears such a striking resemblance to Robert Henri's portrait *Dieguito Roybal* (see page 41) that it is hard to believe that three-quarters of a century divides the two.
Left and right: Today's Pueblo dances are remarkably similar to those witnessed by the early Taos and Santa Fe painters. At left, the Cloud Dance at Santa Clara Pueblo; at right, a dancer in full regalia at the Taos Pueblo Pow-wow.

and to this day works with the abstracted shapes and compositions he began to explore nearly 60 years ago.

It was not the end product, or the style of applying paint, that made a Transcendentalist painting transcendental. It was the experience the artist had behind its creation.

Though seen at first as hair-brained and even destructively dangerous by the more conservative of the early arrivals, the Transcendentalists were gradually embraced by the pioneer painters Blumenschein, Sharp and Couse, among others.

Greatly influenced by the symbolic paintings of the Pueblo peoples, the Transcendentalists advocated painting "ideas" as the Native American painters had been doing since the introduction of paint and paper in the 1830s. These frontal paintings by Hopi and Pueblo Indians greatly excited the conceptually-oriented Bisttram, and he passed his enthusiasm along to the other Transcendentalists.

The mystical, ideological Transcendentalists experimented with vegetarianism, celibacy, sweat lodges and other conceptual approaches to life 30 years before the rest of the country tested those waters in the 1960s. They were the original

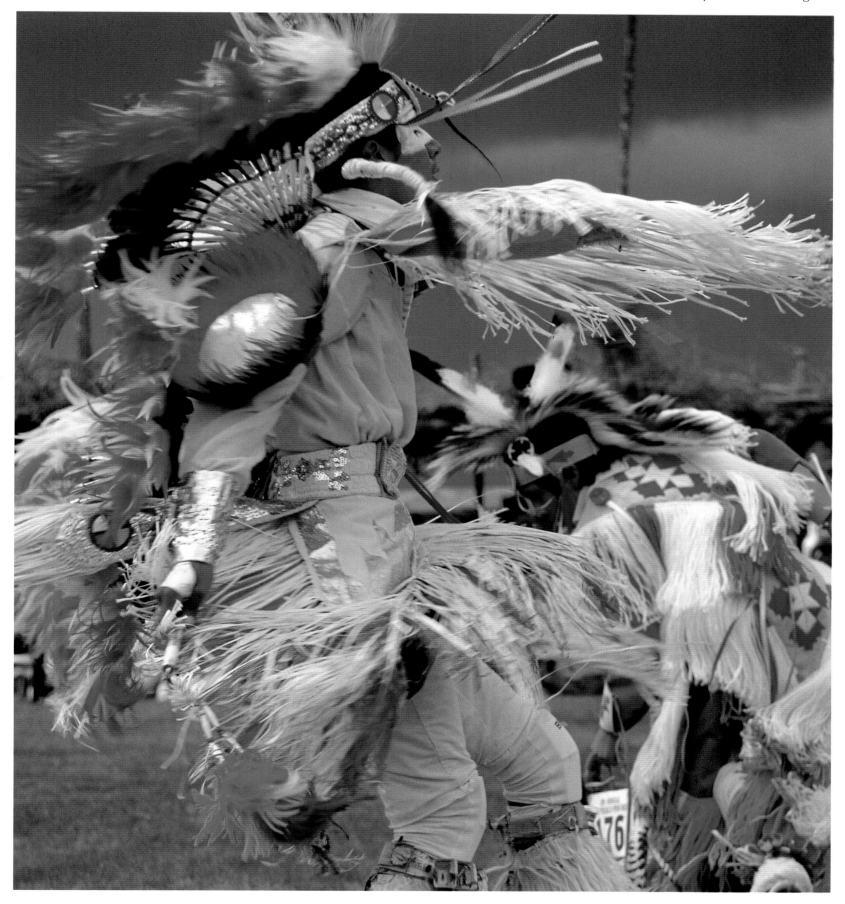

American Bohemians, and they would change the way American painting would evolve.

Unfortunately, the outbreak of World War II cut the Transcendentalists short in terms of an organized group, but the major painters – Bisttram, Lumpkins, Mandelman, Jonson and Morang – all continued to make their homes and to paint in the Southwest. Both Beatrice Mandelman and William Lumpkins are still very much alive and still painting, hip octogenarians heading into the twenty-first century.

Santa Fe today has a population of 55,000 – much larger than the early colony days, but still a small population for a state capital. Taos is considerably smaller and even more isolated than Santa Fe. The area is still an off-the-beaten-track sort of place to visit; there are no international flights to New Mexico, and there is no nonstop access from the East Coast. Still, a large number of tourists pour in every year, some of whom stay, and some of whom stay to pursue their art. There are approximately 1200 working artists in Santa Fe and Taos today, many of whom, like the early painters, are just getting by. Some, however, are nationally recognized, and some are collected by Europeans, whose interest in Southwestern art began in the early colony days.

The art terms that define the history of New York's art evolution are not entirely applicable in the desert Southwest. If one were to ask a Ph.D in Art History to label works from twentieth-century New Mexico according to the terms he or she has learned – Figurative versus Modern, Abstract Expressionist versus Classical Representational, resulting in Post-Modernism – he or she would find that the perfect dialectic for interpreting East Coast and European art simply does not apply to the Southwest.

As the reader will see while viewing the color plates in this book, there is no dialectic going on in the Southwest. Like three trains on parallel tracks, occasionally crossing over, the symbiotically compatible approaches to Southwestern material developed some 100 years ago – Landscape, Figurative, and Abstract Modernist – continue to this day.

The fact that Native American, Hispanic and Anglo artists are all painting now is perhaps the most important change from the early days. Whereas previously only Anglo artists were interpreting scenes of Southwestern life, Native Americans such as Earl Biss are now painting Native American scenes such as Indians on horseback meeting in the woods. T. C. Cannon's portrait *Collector #5* is a Native American's humorous view of the effect of the modern world on his culture. Bernadette Vigil, a member of an old Hispanic family known for its talented artists, is painting the religious processions of the Southwestern Catholic lineage. Many other Native American and Hispanic artists today are also reinterpreting scenes past and present, adding a new dimension to the art community in Santa Fe.

The artists of the late twentieth century are happy in each other's company in Santa Fe. Though some of the contemporary painters have never heard of Transcendentalists or seen their work, they are nevertheless continuing in the tradition of

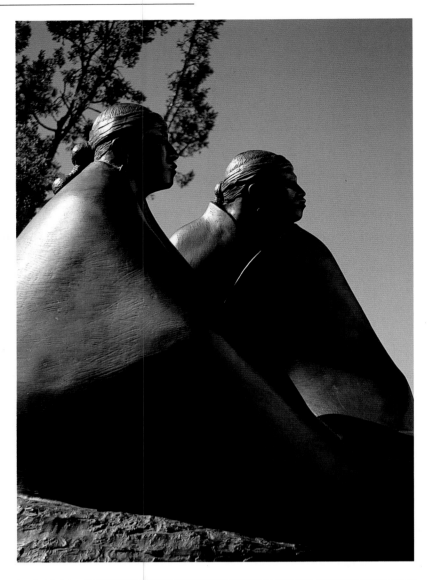

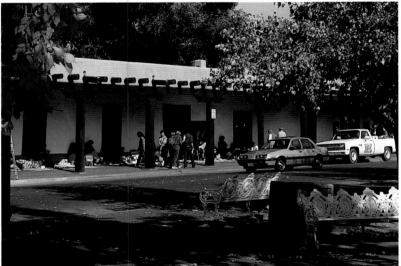

those early aesthetics and mystics. Images of altered states of mind hang on contemporary walls next to an abstract field of color with one floating circular shape, next to a landscape painted on tin. Somehow there is a harmony between these diverse visions inspired by the Southwest.

Soft, architectural pastels by Margaret Nes dazzle the eye of the contemporary observer no less than the graceful architectural paintings Georgia O'Keeffe did 30 years ago. Playful figures dance up a storm, or turn pale with realization, in the genre paintings of Eli Levin and Maurice Burns. The contemporary Southwestern plaza paintings of today are nearly indistinguishable in style from the early versions of the same set-

Left: Internationally collected and extremely prolific, Allan Houser is the premier sculptor of the Southwest. His work, combining a Modernist concern for shape with realistic portraiture, broke the barrier of what was defined as Native American art. This piece is displayed outside the Wheelwright Museum in Santa Fe.

Right and below right: Bob Houzous, *Border Crossing*, 1991, painted steel, 8 × 12 × 14 ft., Rettig.y Martinez Gallery, Santa Fe, NM. The son of Allan Houser, Bob Houzous is also one of the Southwest's best-known sculptors. His 6400-lb. piece *Border Crossing* depicts a barbed-wire barricade on the front (right), and a serene blue sky over an empty desert-scape on the back (below right). Any border between countries or no literal border at all, it represents the very essence of the phenomenon of a border.

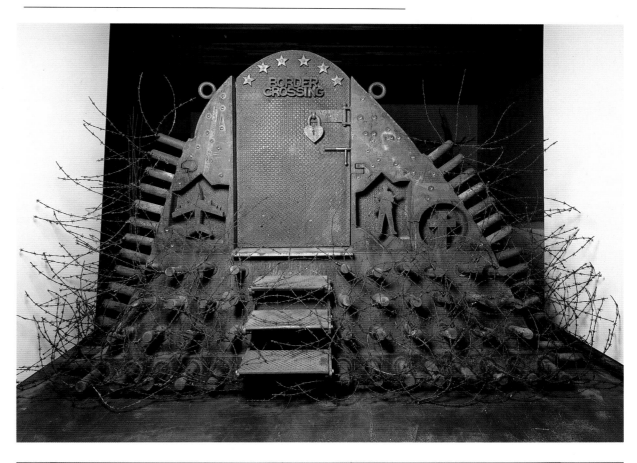

Left: The Palace of the Governors on the plaza in Santa Fe is the longest-occupied governmental building in the United States. The site of the 1680 Pueblo uprising, for the past century only Native Americans have sold their works under the portal. Some of the finest Native American arts and crafts in the Southwest can be found here.

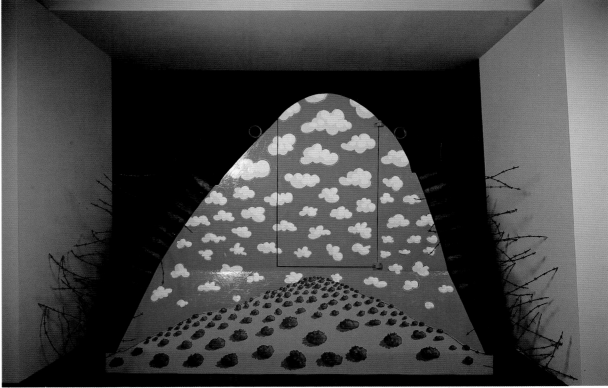

ting. There is a fine continuum, an undeniable sense of history in Santa Fe art.

Many artists in Santa Fe and Taos are also producing sculptures which are redefining the traditions of the Southwest. The wealth of flat artwork from the area has precluded the inclusion of sculpture in the color plates of this book, but such artists as Allan Houser, Bob Houzous (Houser's son), Luis Jimenez, Bruce Nauman, and Bruce and Presley LaFountain are sculptors of international renown. Other sculptors such as Rachel Dutton, James Marshall and Tony Price, influenced by the proximity of the Los Alamos nuclear research facility, are producing a unique brand of "eco-art" that stands in contrast to the soft, traditional shapes of the desert Southwest. At the other extreme, Native Americans continue to make the beautiful pottery characteristic of their tribes, using techniques passed down from generation to generation. The richness and diversity of art being produced in Santa Fe and Taos today is truly staggering.

Though everyone in the modern world wants to be original and new, that is not the entire point of Southwestern art. Each person who picks up a paintbrush today has the opportunity to bring something new to the canvas, but the multicultural and stylistic diversity of the Southwestern tradition will appear on the palette whether the painter is aware of it or not.

THE TAOS SOCIETY AND EARLY TAOS ART

In 1898, two young illustrators, Ernest Blumenschein and Bert Geer Phillips, traveled from Paris (where they had been studying under Joseph Henry Sharp at L'Académie Julian) to Denver, where they rented a wagon with the plan of making a sketching tour from Colorado to Mexico. Inspired by Sharp, who was one of the first Anglo artists to paint the West, Blumenschein and Phillips headed south on rutted roads, with paint and supplies, in spite of the fact that neither had ever been a wrangler. Just 20 miles outside of Taos, where Sharp had his home base, one of their wagon wheels broke and they soon found themselves in their teacher's adobe home. With that broken wagon wheel, the gathering of the early Taos painters began.

By the time Blumenschein and Phillips arrived, Joseph Sharp had been in the West for 15 years. Sharp first visited New Mexico in 1883, returning to Taos between cross-Atlantic trips to Paris and horseback trips to his summer headquarters at Pine Ridge, South Dakota, where he painted *The Stoic*, one of his best-known works, depicting a Sioux Sundance ritual.

Between 1880 and 1893, Sharp spent his summers among the most feared of the Native American tribes, the Montana Crow and the South Dakota Sioux. Due to a childhood illness, Joseph Sharp was completely deaf, and it may have been this handicap that enabled him to return repeatedly to the war zone of the Sioux (the horrible massacre by the Cavalry at Wounded Knee, only miles from Pine Ridge, happened in 1890). Essentially mute but very capable of hand signal communication, and with an ability to paint comprehending portrayals of the sometimes brutal rituals he witnessed, Sharp was granted an unheard-of entry into the secret enclaves of the still warring West.

After moving to Taos, Bert Phillips soon became known for Native American portraits similar to, but more pastoral than, Sharp's. Phillips found a kinship with the Native Americans, noting that they "worship all things beautiful."

In 1909 Blumenschein married fellow painter Mary Shepard Greene in Paris, and they eventually settled in Taos. Ernest's genre paintings of the Pueblo dancers grew more hallucinogenic and frontal, while his wife Mary Greene painted symbolist images.

In 1902 another internationally known illustrator, E. I. Couse, arrived in Taos. Already a spiritual initiate in Native American ceremonies, and a close friend to many Native American peoples, Couse's work focused on intimate portraits of the Taos Indians.

W. Herbert "Buck" Dunton's arrival in 1912 further expanded the group of Taos artists. Known for his portraits of cowboys and farmers, Dunton explored the life of the homesteaders in large oils that emphasized the vastness of Western landscapes.

Oscar Berninghaus first traveled west in 1899 on a commission for the Denver and Rio Grande Railroad, and found that the people and the light profoundly changed the way that he painted. He returned to Taos from St. Louis every summer, and finally moved there. Berninghaus was invited to become one of the six founding members of the Taos Society of Artists at its inception in 1915.

Victor Higgins moved to Taos in 1914 and joined the artists' group in 1917. Today considered one of the most outstanding of all the early painters, Higgins was capable of flooding Native American portraits with thickly painted light that is as much about medium as it is about content. In one of his most famous pieces, *Pueblo of Taos*, orange and red Indian blankets cut across the picture plane in designs that echo both Japanese woodblock prints and early Hopi gouaches.

Walter Ufer, a student of the Munich school, also joined the Taos Society of Artists in 1917. Extremely prolific and capable of depicting sadly profound themes while using a lighthearted, therapeutically beautiful technique, Ufer was a master. Ufer's *Hunger* is one of the most contemporary-looking of the early Taos works.

Catharine Critcher was a respected artist in the European avant-garde before she moved to New Mexico, and had studied under the same teachers as Matisse. Critcher was very interested in symbolism, as well as abstraction, and her work preceded that of Georgia O'Keeffe in such experimentation.

E. Martin Hennings visited Walter Ufer in Taos in 1917 and returned permanently in 1921. Hennings was known for capturing the high desert's brilliant light and the elegant dignity of the Southwestern Pueblo people.

Kenneth Adams, the last member elected to the Taos Society of Artists, in 1926, moved to Taos in 1924. Adams had studied under Andrew Dasburg at the Art Students League in New York, had done the mandatory stint in Europe, and had spent a brief time working with the Mexican muralists Orozco and Sequieros.

Seven thousand people lived in the Taos valley by the 1920s, but only a few hundred of those were English speaking, and many of them were artists. In 1927, the Taos Society of Artists disbanded because its original aim of setting up exhibitions was no longer necessary. The artists themselves were receiving more offers than they could fill, and though Taos was still isolated, painters and other Anglo visitors were pouring in almost daily.

Leon Gaspard, a Russian painter who was badly wounded in World War I, went to Taos in 1918. Gaspard, who used paint applied in fast, thick strokes to capture remarkable details of motion and light, chose Taos to recover from his war wounds, and essentially made it his home base.

The Honorable Dorothy Brett, affectionately known as Lady Brett, was already an established painter in Great Britain when she ventured to New Mexico in 1924 with D. H. Lawrence and his wife. Brett abstracted the ritualistic Pueblo dances into circles of feather-shaped figures. Her flower-shaped genre paintings nearly escape the representational altogether and cross over into the abstract, something many painters soon to come to New Mexico would do.

Andrew Dasburg moved to New Mexico in 1918 and was the first truly Modernist Southwestern painter. Dasburg saw the possibility of combining Cubist perspectives with the abstracted shapes characteristic of the New Mexican desert, and in doing so, took Cubism farther than anyone else in the Southwest. A fundamentally important American painter whose work was featured at the Armory Show in 1913, Dasburg eventually replaced Blumenschein as the dominating mentor in the Taos colony. Dasburg painted hundreds of canvases, and painted every day up until his death in 1979 at the age of 94.

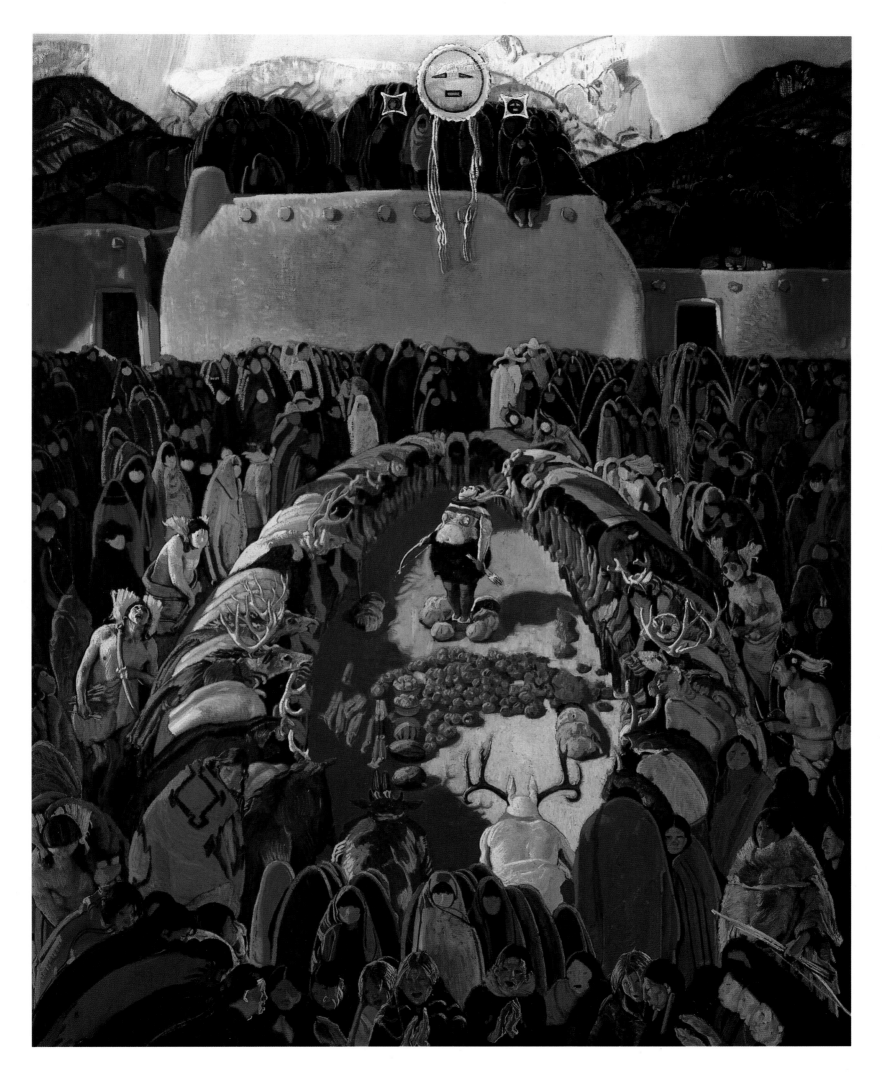

Ernest L. Blumenschein (1874-1960)
Moon, Morning and Evening Star
1922, oil on canvas, 50 × 40 in.
Thomas Gilcrease Institute, Tulsa, OK

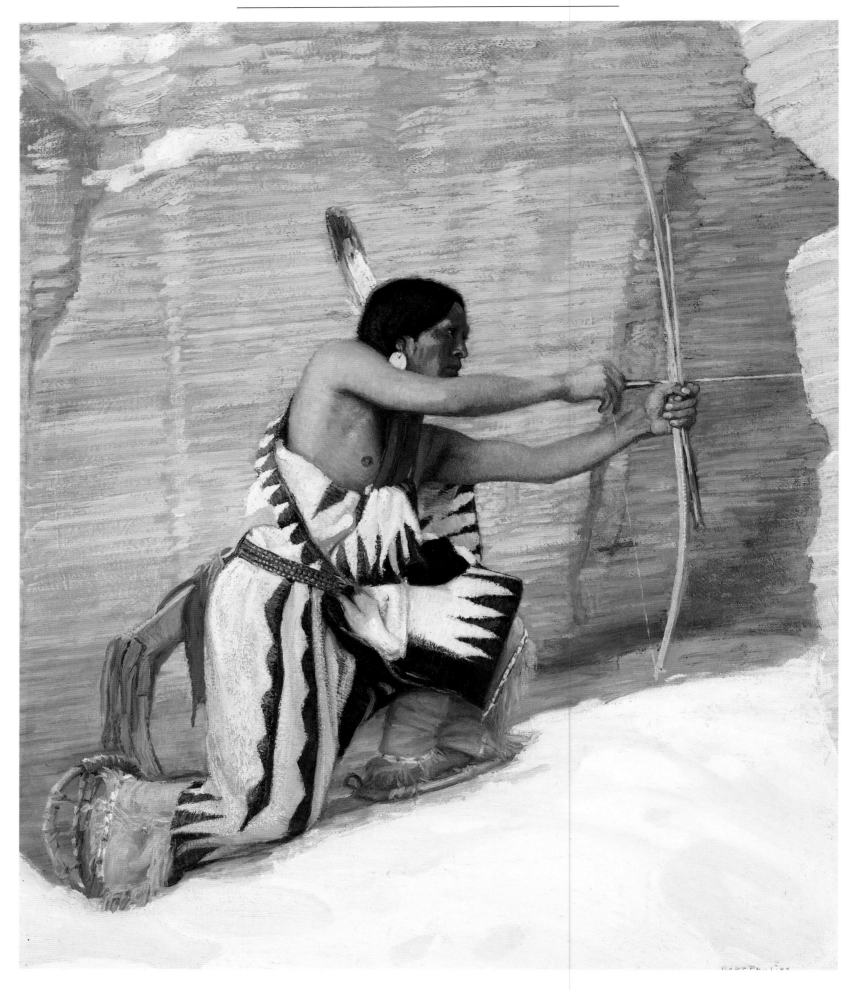

Bert Geer Phillips (1868-1956)
Kneeling Indian
n.d., oil on canvas, 29 × 24 in.
Photo courtesy of the Gerald Peters Gallery, Santa Fe, NM

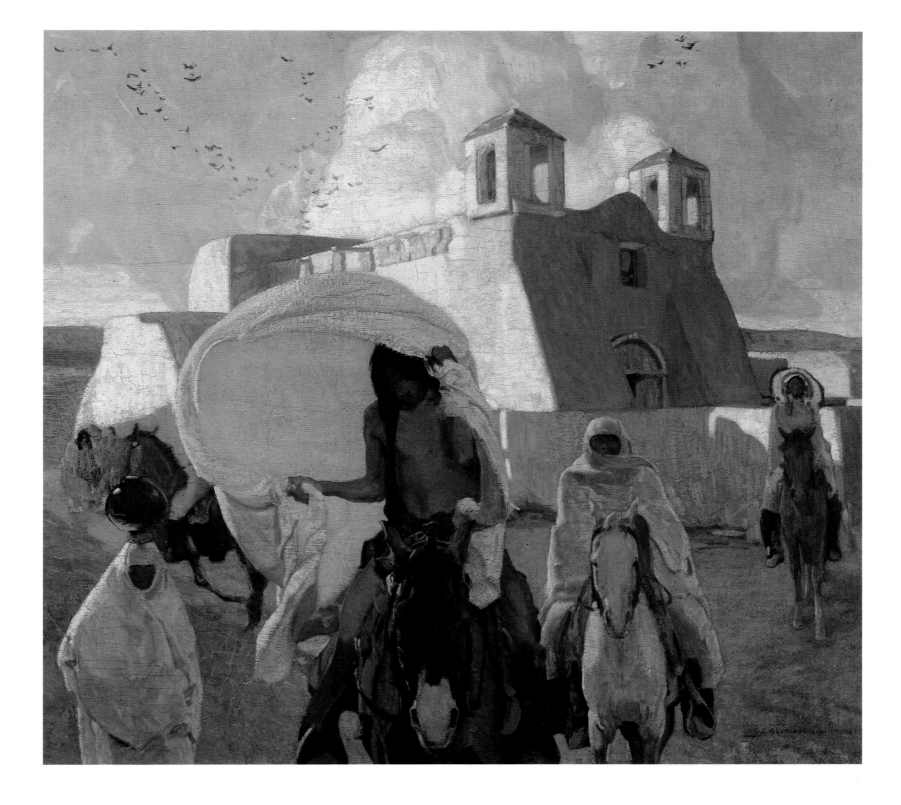

ERNEST L. BLUMENSCHEIN
Church at Ranchos de Taos
Before 1917, oil on canvas, 45 × 47 in.
Courtesy of the Anschutz Collection, Denver, CO
Photo by James O. Milmoe

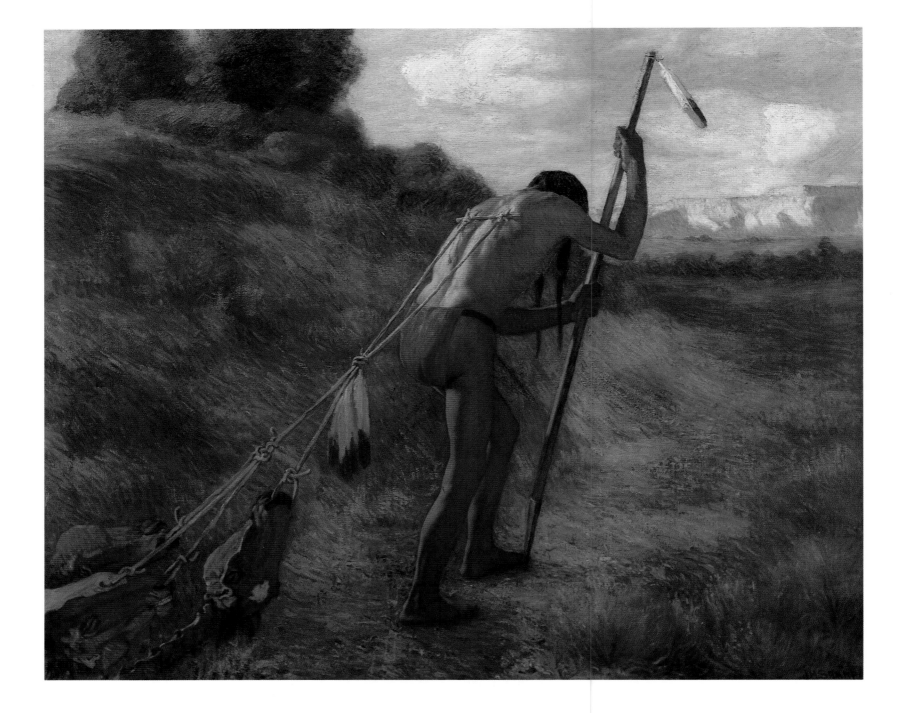

Joseph Henry Sharp (1859-1953)
The Stoic
1914, oil on canvas, 52½ × 61½ in.
Gift of the Artist, 1917
Museum of Fine Arts, Museum of New Mexico, Santa Fe, NM

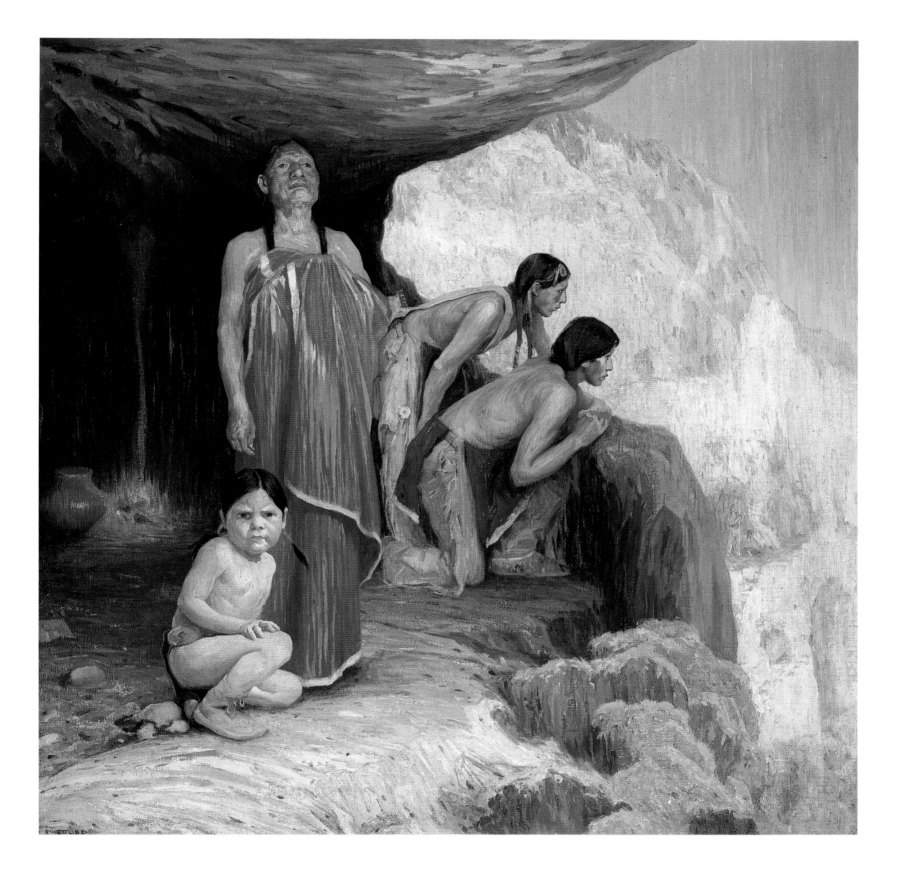

EANGER IRVING COUSE (1866-1936)
Sun Worshipers
c. 1919, oil on canvas, 60 × 60 in.
Photo courtesy of the Gerald Peters Gallery, Santa Fe, NM

VICTOR HIGGINS (1884-1949)
Pueblo of Taos
Before 1927, oil on canvas, 43½ × 53½ in.
Courtesy of the Anschutz Collection, Denver, CO
Photo by James O. Milmoe

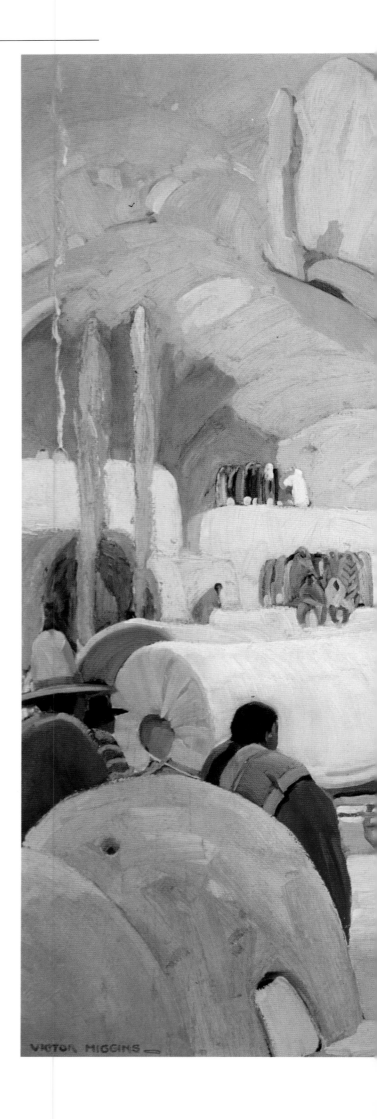

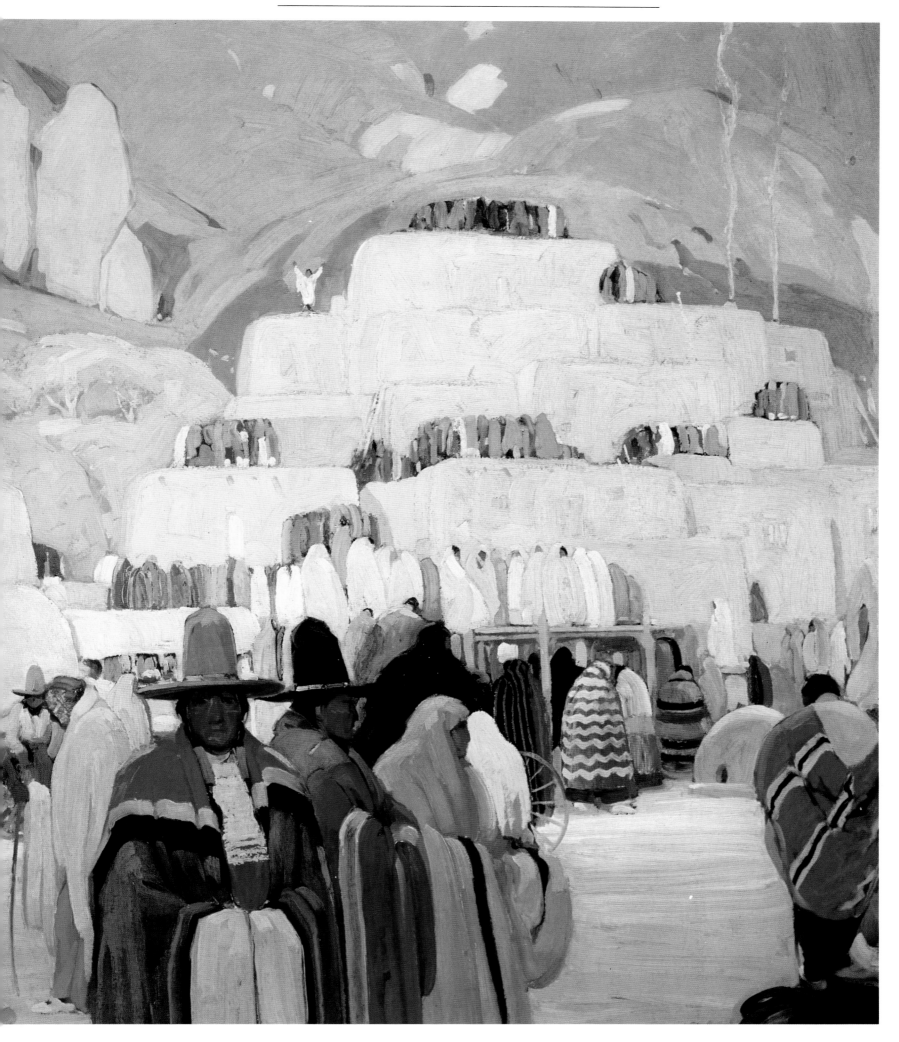

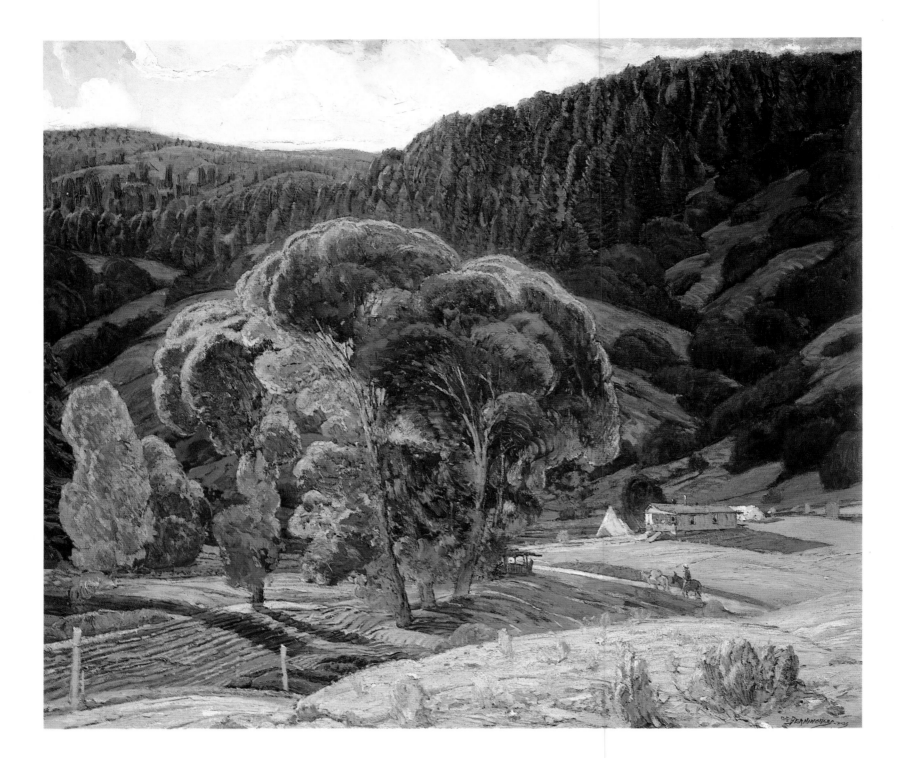

Oscar E. Berninghaus (1874-1952)
On the Road to Taos
n.d., oil on canvas, 25 × 39¼ in.
Photo courtesy of the Gerald Peters Gallery, Santa Fe, NM

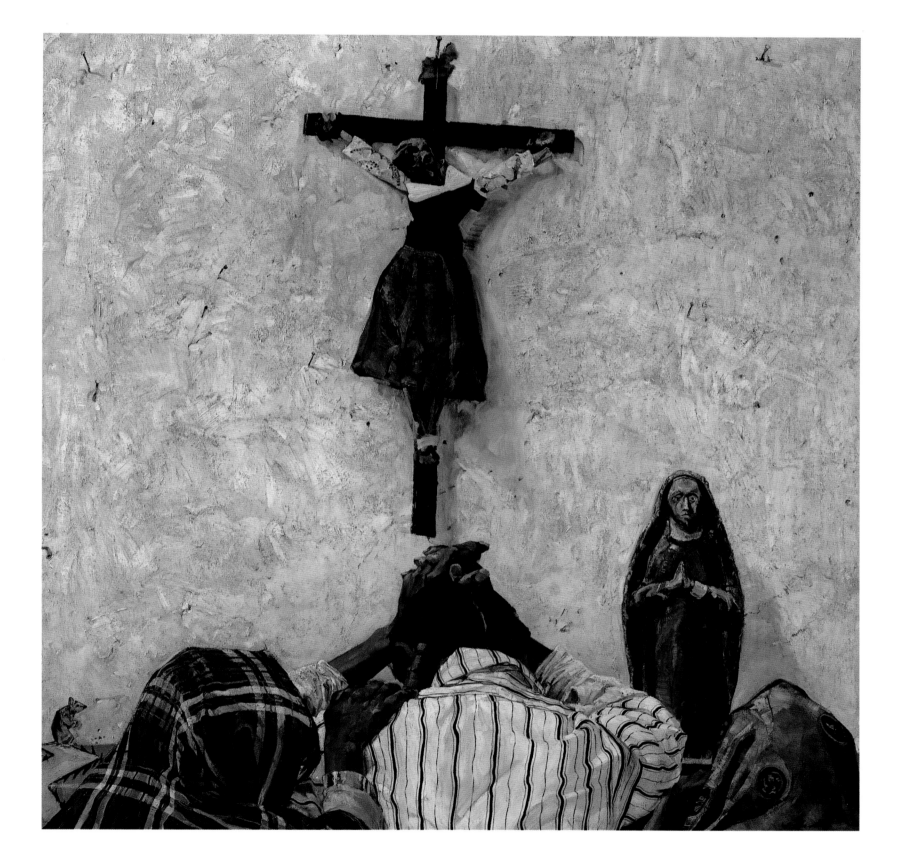

Walter Ufer (1876-1936)
Hunger
n.d., oil on canvas, 50½ × 50¼ in.
Thomas Gilcrease Institute, Tulsa, OK

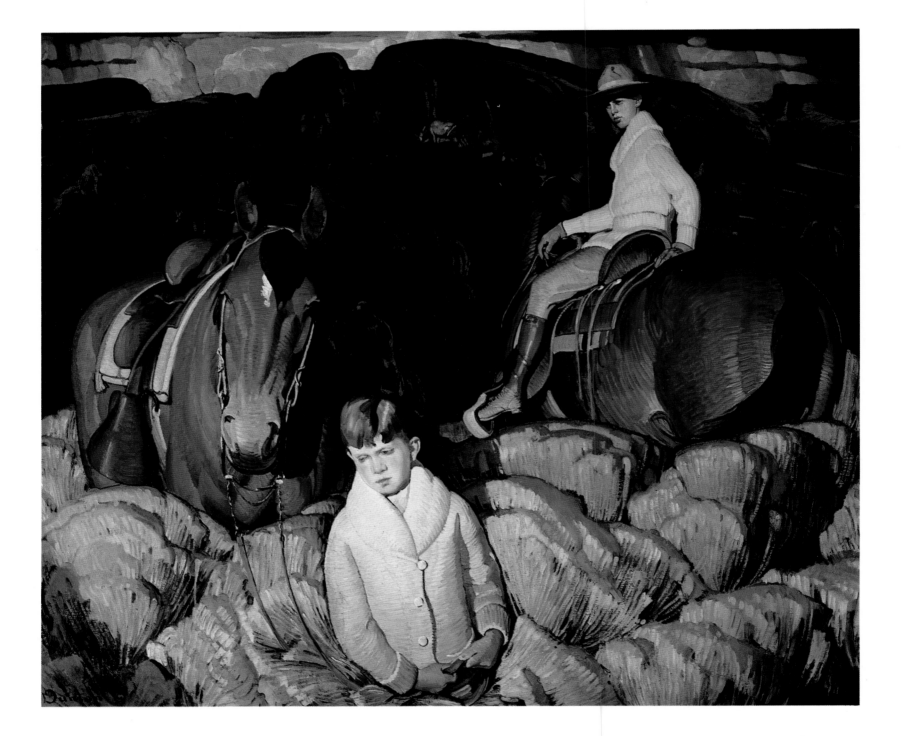

W. HERBERT DUNTON (1878-1936)
My Children
1922, oil on canvas, 50 × 60 in.
Gift of Anonymous Donor, 1927
Museum of Fine Arts, Museum of New Mexico, Santa Fe, NM

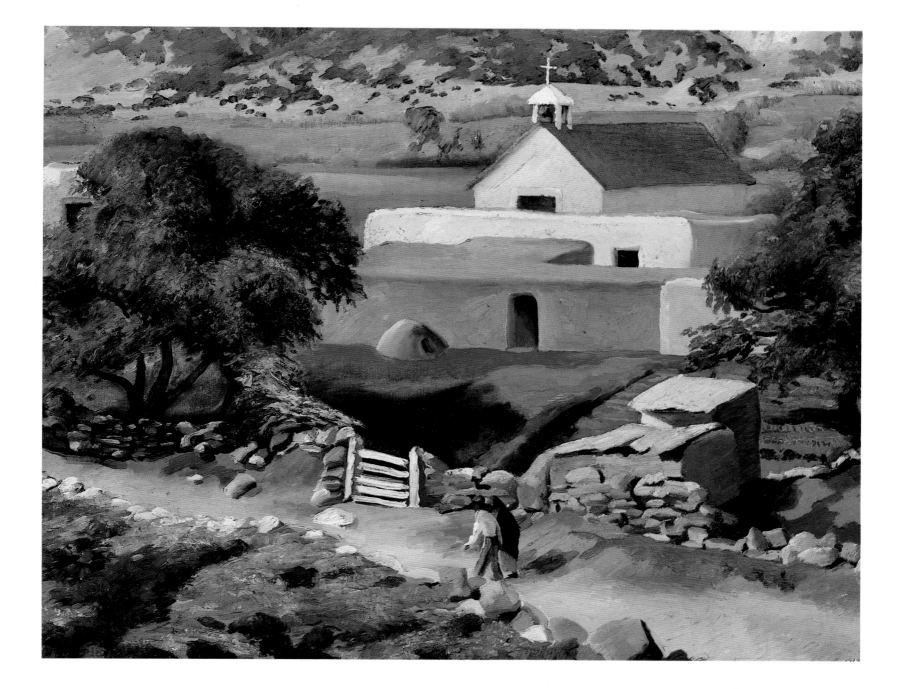

Kenneth M. Adams (1897-1966)
The Mission Church
Before 1925, oil on canvas, 20 × 25 in.
Courtesy of the Anschutz Collection, Denver, CO
Photo by James O. Milmoe

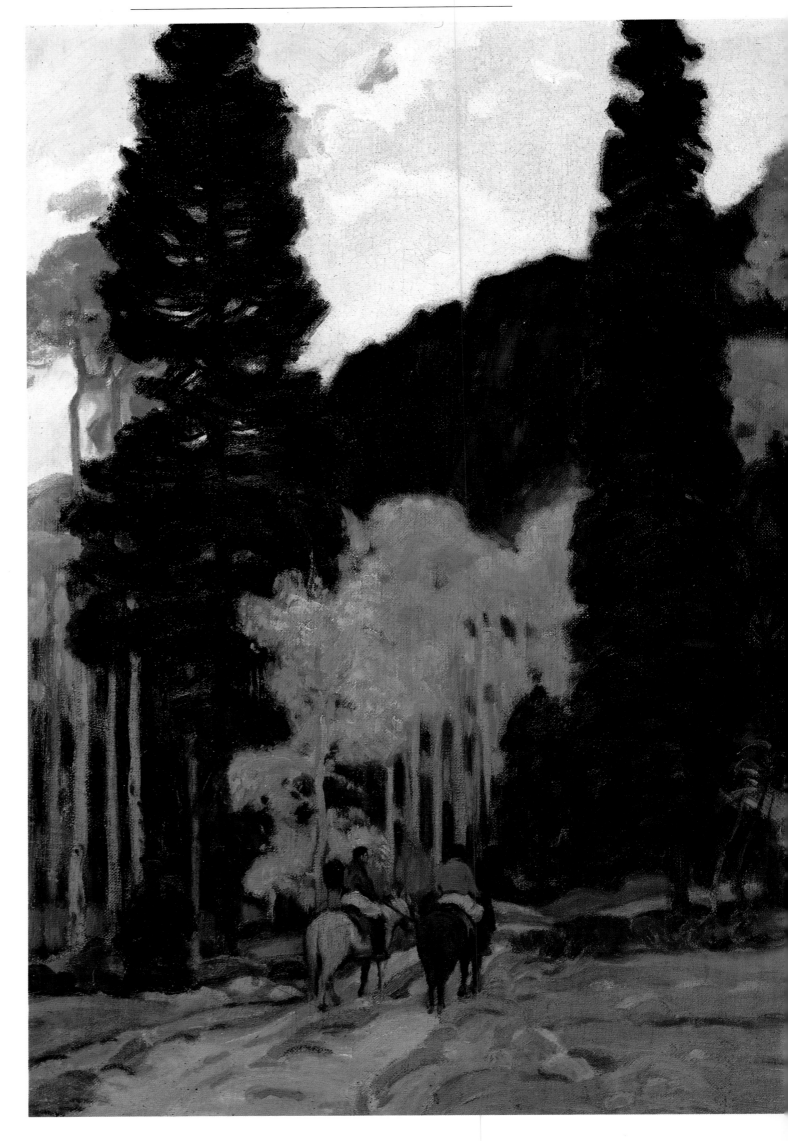

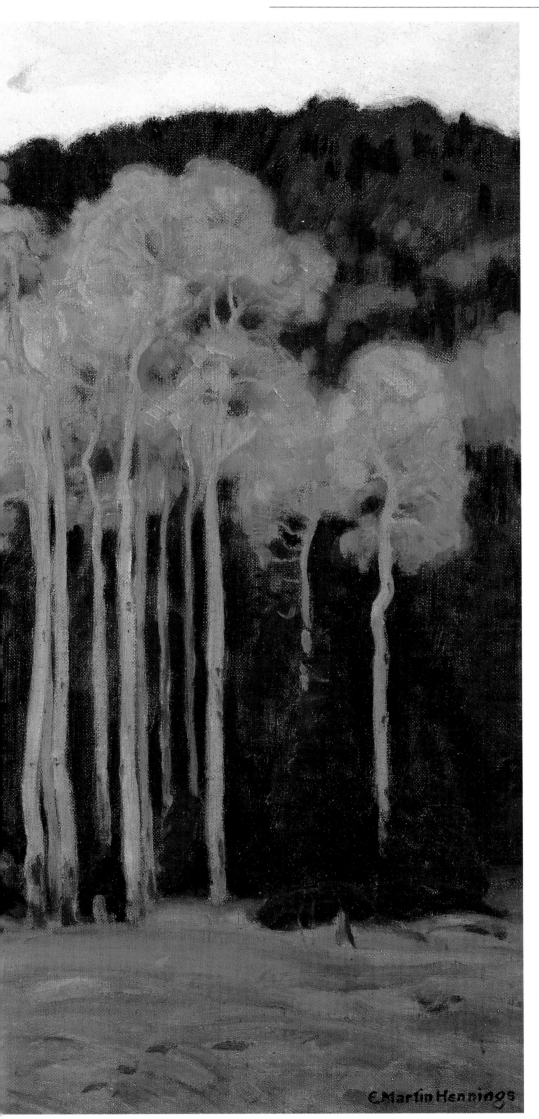

E. Martin Hennings (1886-1956)
Taos Indian Riders
c. 1935-1945, oil on canvas, 20 × 24 in.
*Photo courtesy of the Gerald Peters Gallery,
    Santa Fe, NM*

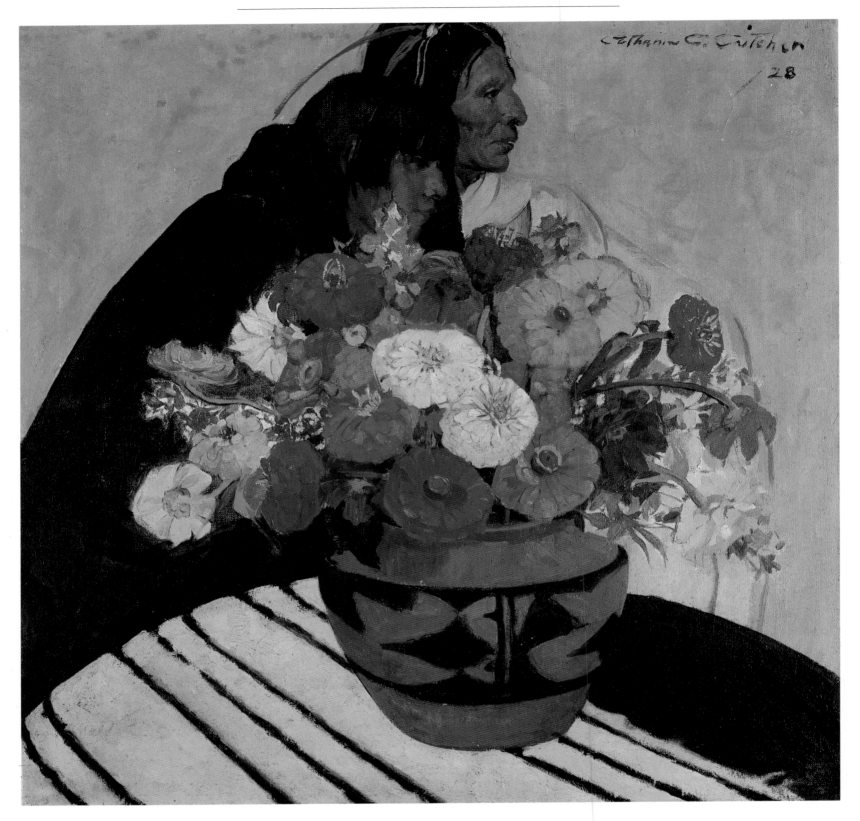

Catharine C. Critcher (1868-1964)
Pueblo Family
1928, oil on canvas, 30 × 30¼ in.
*Collection of the Eiteljorg Museum of American
    Indian and Western Art, Indianapolis, IN*

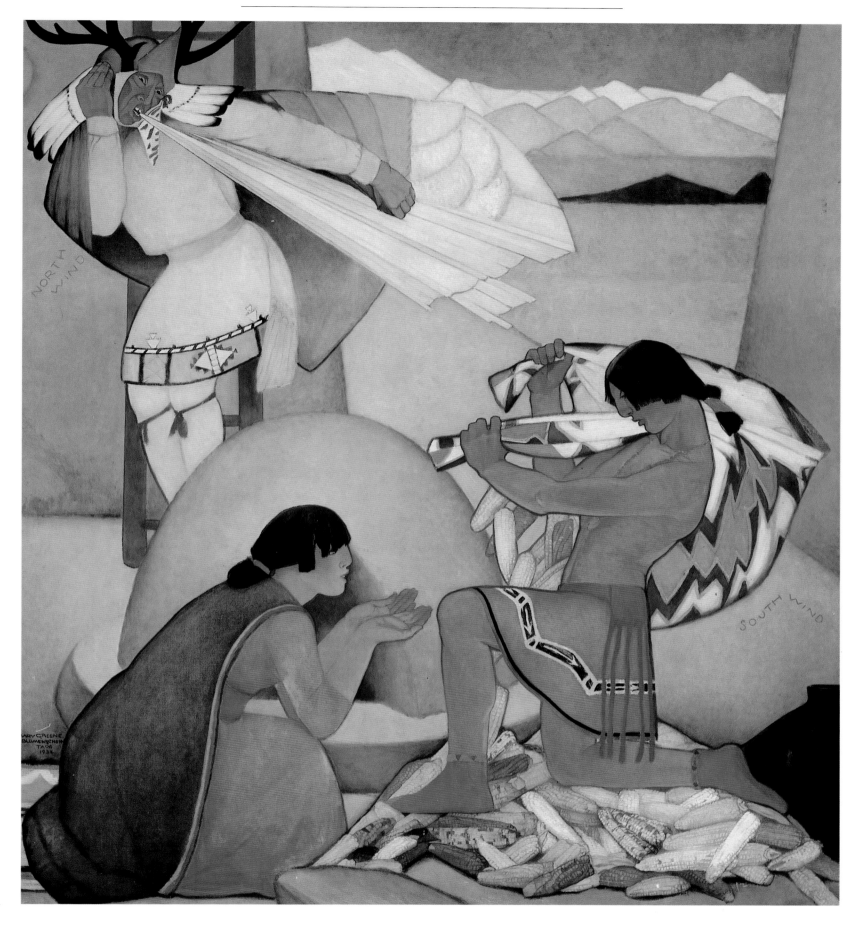

Mary Greene Blumenschein (1868-1958)
Acoma Legend
1932, oil on canvas, 50⅛ × 45 in.
Gift of the Lovelace Medical Foundation
The Albuquerque Museum, NM
Photo by Damian Andrus

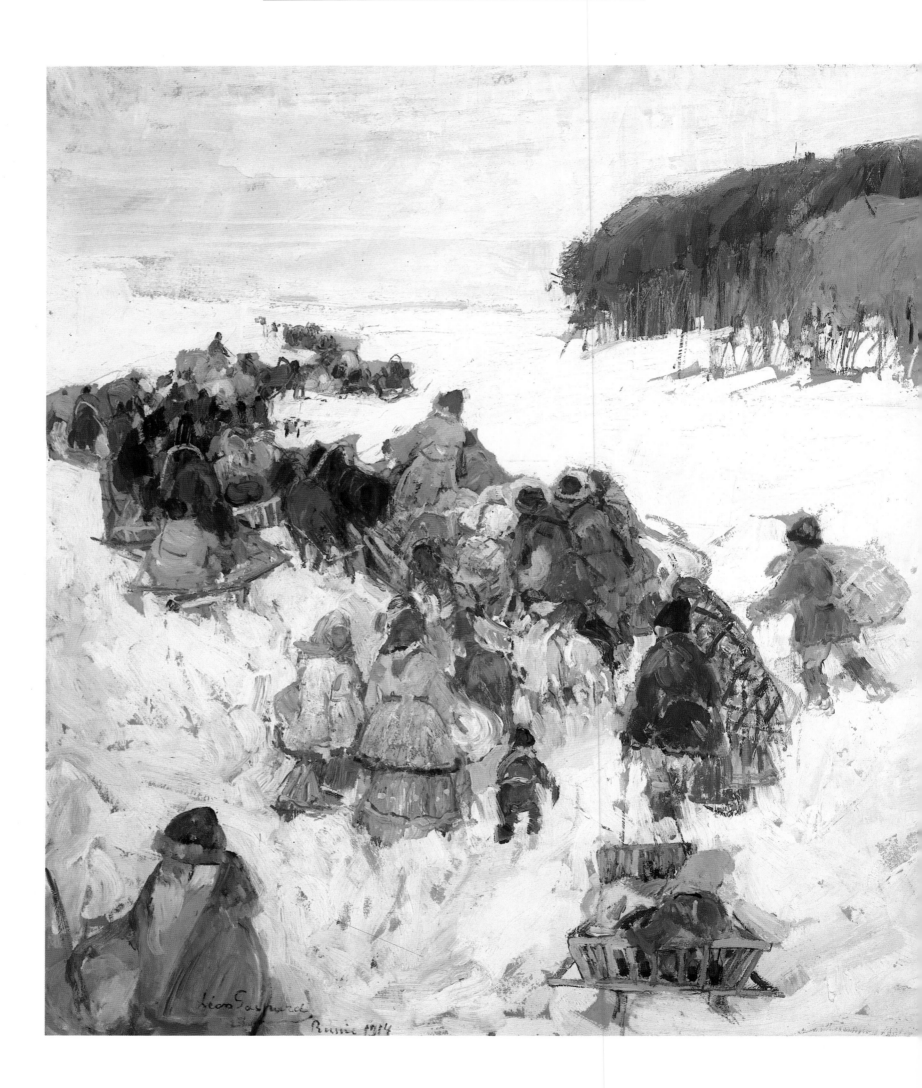

LEON GASPARD (1882-1964)
Snow Scene
n.d., oil on canvas, 22 × 26 in.
Photo courtesy of the Gerald Peters Gallery, Santa Fe, NM

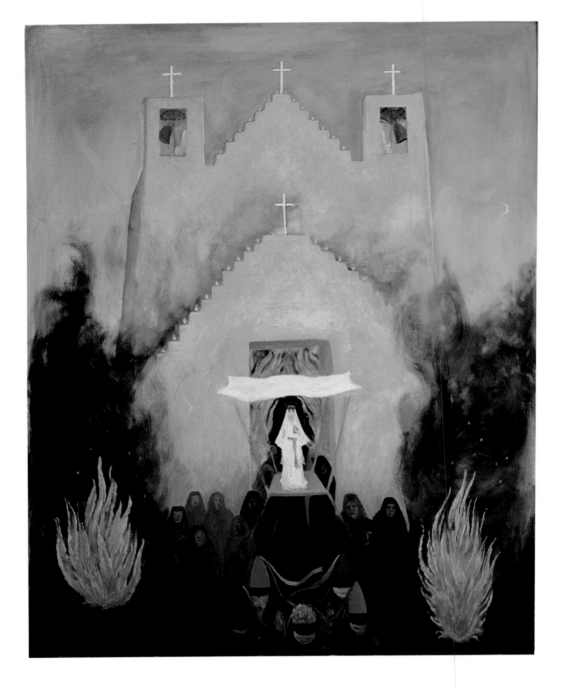

The Hon. Dorothy Brett (1883-1977)
Christmas Eve Fires, Taos Pueblo
1961, oil on canvas, 60 × 48 in.
Collection of the Harwood Foundation, Taos, NM

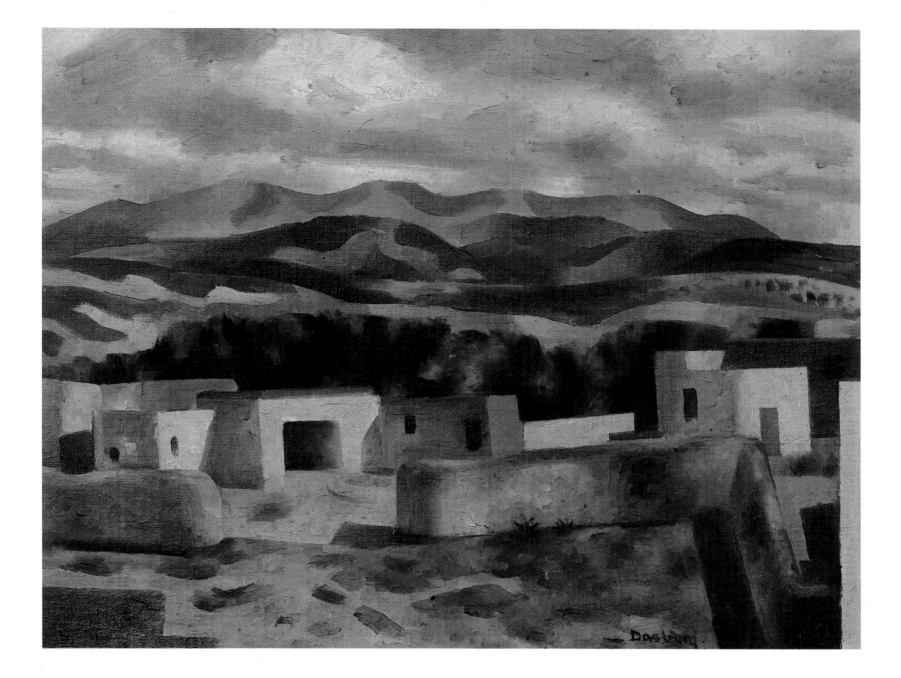

Andrew Dasburg (1887-1979)
My Gate on the Camino
1928, oil on canvas, 13 × 16 in.
Gift of Mrs. R. J. Erickson, 1964
Museum of Fine Arts, Museum of New Mexico, Santa Fe, NM

LOS CINCO PINTORES AND EARLY SANTA FE ART

By 1919, when Randall Davey and John Sloan arrived in New Mexico in their race car, the wagon trails had become roads – after a fashion. The legendary trip from New York took six weeks of driving on muddy, rutted roads, using a quart of oil a day and a gallon of gas every four miles. The Simplex's obsolete tires took a beating, and finally one went flat past repair in a tiny town in northern New Mexico. Fortunately the painters and their wives weren't far from a railroad station, and they were able to climb aboard the train (car and all) and soon reach their destination of Santa Fe. Their story is remarkably similar to that of Blumen-schein and Phillips, who arrived in Taos a couple of decades earlier – a transportation break-down initiating an artists' colony.

Only a decade – and hundreds of canvases – later, the early Santa Fe renaissance was at its peak. In 1929, while most of the country was struggling, the painters in Santa Fe were more prolific than ever. While the rest of the West was still untamed and "un-civilized," Santa Fe and Taos were cosmopolitan and inter-national. In Santa Fe, modern art was no shock, but an exciting and very much alive theater for painters ready to break the rules.

Józef Bakoś, Will Shuster, Walter Mruk, Willard Nash, and Fremont Ellis formed Los Cinco Pintores in 1921, advocating that modern art was for the common man. As Bakoś wrote in their initial statement of purpose, "The concept is that art is universal, that it sings to the peasant laborer as well as to the connoisseur."

The young Cinco Pintores banded together not only for ex-hibition purposes, but also for political purposes. Like their con-temporaries in Taos, the Santa Fe painters were involved with the Pueblo peoples, and when in 1922 the Bursum Indian Bill threatened to relocate the Pueblos, the artists went to Washing-ton and joined a successful lobby against the bill. They also donated paintings to auctions to raise money for the Indian milk fund and to feed Indian livestock during draught years.

Rowdy in behavior, and known for their nightly parties, drink-ing bootleg liquor during Prohibition, Los Cinco Pintores were experimental in every way possible. Though their manifestos clearly advocated abstracted work, they actually painted in many styles, including landscape, still life and portraiture.

At first at odds with their more representational predecessors, soon the Southwestern tradition of tolerance and mutual respect took over and before long Blumenschein and Dasburg from Taos, and Frank Applegate and John Sloan from Santa Fe, were paint-ing in the same studios, drinking Bakoś's homebrew beer, and sharing ideas. The result was that figurative painters became more abstract, and abstractionists were exploring the natural shapes of the desert landscape.

One such abstract painter to spend a good deal of time in New Mexico during the height of the Santa Fe colony was the inter-nationally acclaimed artist Marsden Hartley, who prior to coming to the Southwest painted purely abstract works influenced by Kandinsky, the European Cubists, the Dadaists and the Post-Impressionists. His discovery of shapes in the desert that were more abstract than anything his imagination had created drew him back to a kind of realism that rejected the abstract mandate from Europe. After his stay in Santa Fe and Taos in 1918-19, Hart-ley's painting changed forever. For decades to come he painted the Southwest from memory.

Robert Henri spent many productive years in Santa Fe, and Randall Davey and John Sloan both settled there permanently shortly after their arrival in 1919, yet all of these very important early twentieth century American painters are often categorized as East Coast artists. This is not surprising when one considers that from 1900 to 1930, the Southwestern colonies were in-timately connected to the East Coast. In New York, Robert Henri was the mentor and founding member of the controversial group which was dubbed "The Ashcan School" by hostile critics, even though they called themselves The Eight. The group, which also included Henri's students John Sloan, George Bellows and Edward Hopper, held an exhibition in protest against the con-servative National Academy of Design at the Macbeth Gallery in 1908, and continued to show together on a loosely organized basis into the 1930s.

Randall Davey was also a student of Henri's, and for a while painted the working class subjects of the Ashcan School, though he turned to landscape and portraiture after moving to Santa Fe. Henri, Davey, and Sloan were all included in the 1913 Armory Show, and remained life-long friends.

Alfred Morang was, perhaps, the most active, diplomatic and multi-talented of all the early Santa Fe painters. Morang applied paint with a thickness that results in an almost hallucinogenic effect, and like his friends, the Ashcan painters, he often painted ordinary people and scenes that were sometimes considered to verge on the vulgar – only, instead of New York genres, Morang painted Canyon Road scenes. *The Lady of the Evening* is a Morang classic, thickly painted on a sized workshirt. A fire in his studio tragically took Morang's life in 1958 and destroyed dozens of his paintings.

In 1929, Henriette Wyeth, the sister of Andrew Wyeth and daughter of illustrator N. C. Wyeth, and her new husband Peter Hurd, moved to New Mexico. Hurd was well-known for his Hop-per-like realist scenes of the West, while Wyeth is best known for her still lifes and portraits.

B. J. O. Nordfeldt from Sweden, Henry Balink from Holland, and Gustave Baumann from Germany were three émigrés to find their way to Santa Fe, each interpreting the Native American cul-ture that they found there with Post-Impressionistic perspectives, light and images that often verged on the abstract.

William Penhallow Henderson, who was born in Massachu-setts but grew up in Texas and Kansas, was fascinated with the exotic processions of the Southwest's Penitentes. Carl Sandburg, who visited Mabel Dodge Luhan while Henderson was painting there, wrote, "It is my guess that Henderson did these paintings because the spirit of the inevitable sat on him."

Carlos Vierra was one of the first painters to move to Santa Fe, arriving from California in 1904 to recuperate from failing health. Vierra dedicated his life to photographing and painting the Southwest's Pueblos, Spanish missions and churches. He was much beloved and respected in Santa Fe, and a bronze plaque commemorating him is inlaid in the sidewalk outside of the Museum of Fine Arts, in Santa Fe.

ROBERT HENRI (1865-1929)
Portrait of Dieguito Roybal of San Ildefonso, NM
1916, oil on canvas, 65⅜ × 40⁷⁄₁₆ in.
Gift of the Artist, 1916
Museum of Fine Arts, Museum of New Mexico, Santa Fe, NM

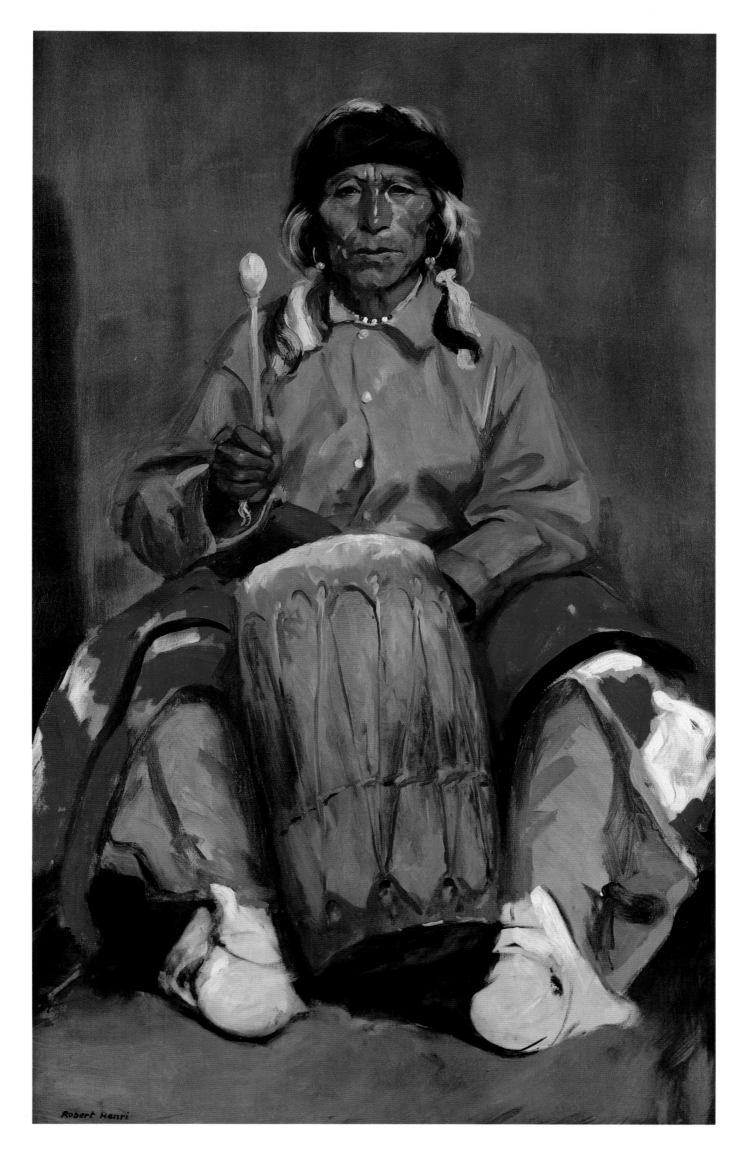

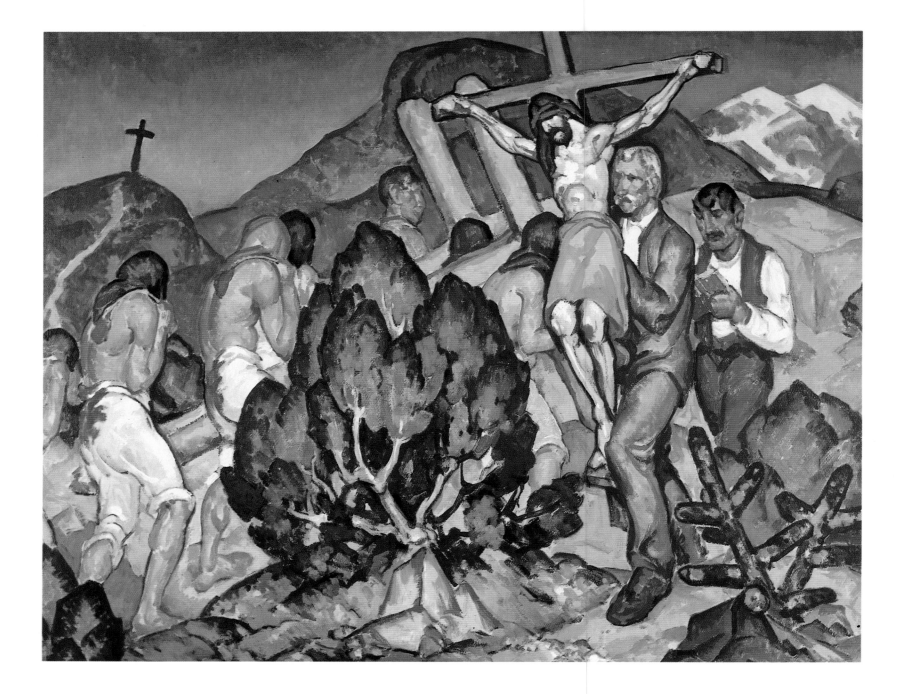

WILLIAM PENHALLOW HENDERSON (1877-1943)
Penitente Procession (Holy Week in New Mexico)
1919, oil on panel, 32 × 40 in.
Gift of Mrs. Edgar L. Rossin, daughter of the Artist, 1952
Museum of Fine Arts, Museum of New Mexico, Santa Fe, NM

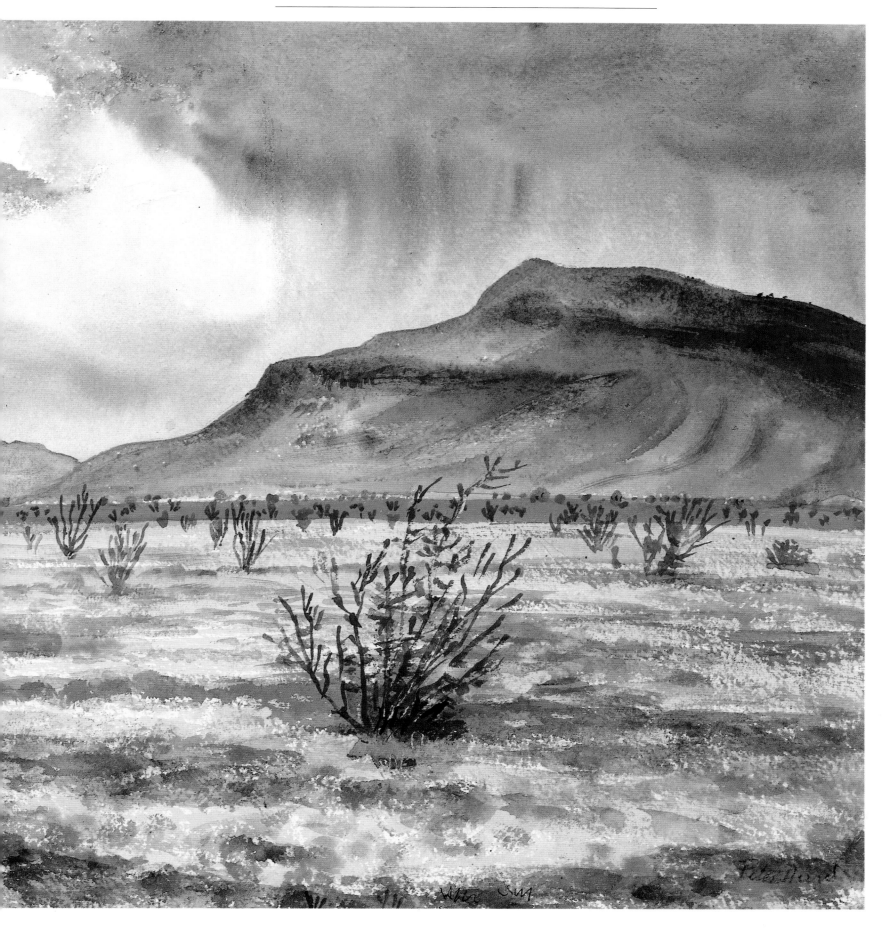

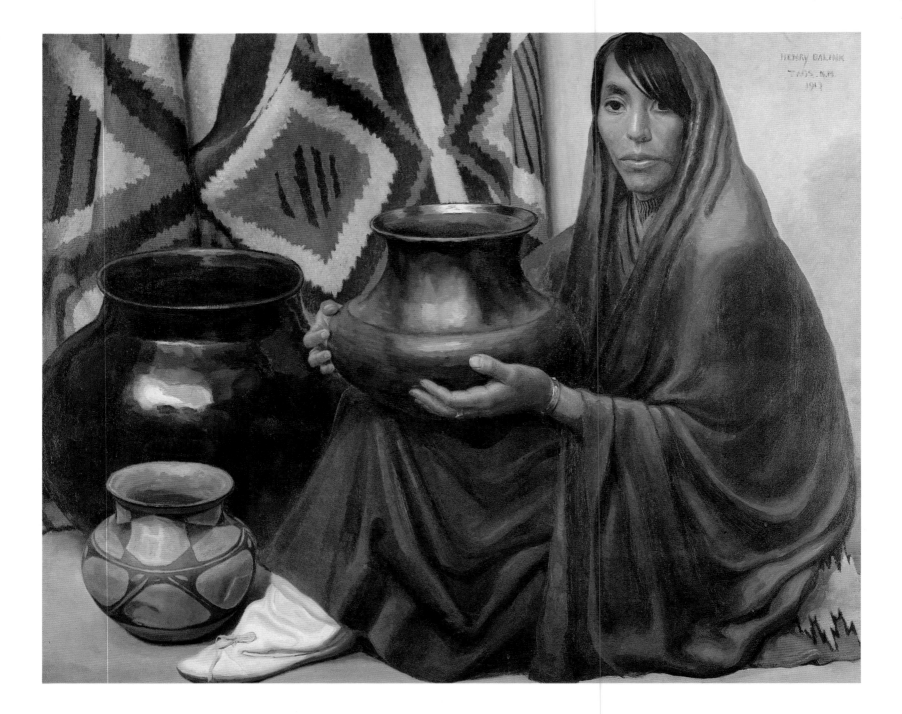

Henry Balink (1882-1963)
Pueblo Pottery
1917, oil on canvas, 27 × 33 in.
Gift of Herman C. and Bina L. Ilfeld, 1977
Museum of Fine Arts, Museum of New Mexico, Santa Fe, NM

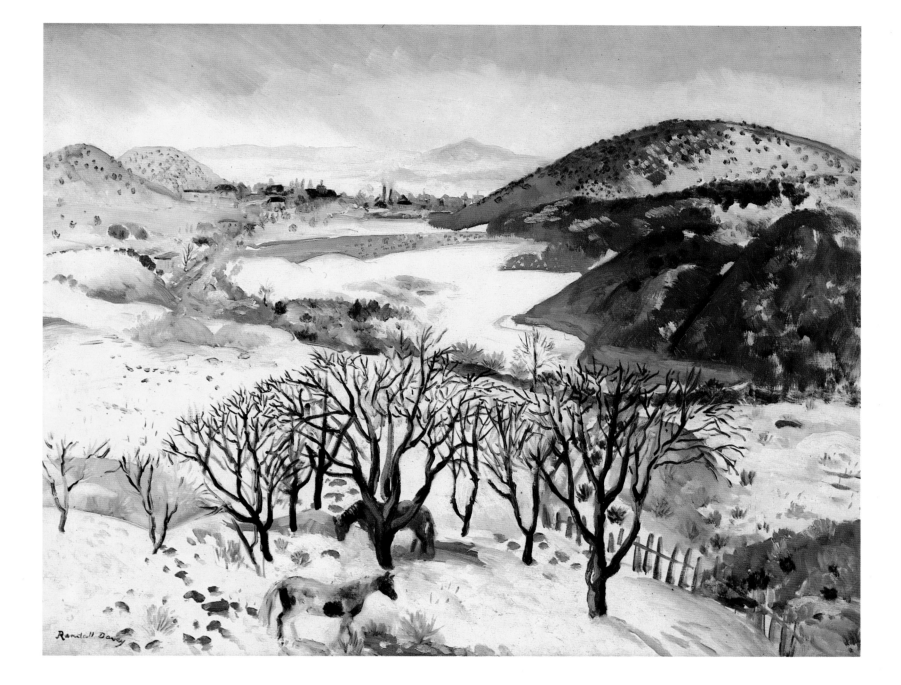

RANDALL DAVEY (1887-1964)
Winter Landscape – New Mexico
1923, oil on canvas, 26 × 32 in.
Purchased with funds from the Museum of New Mexico Foundation
    and Mrs. E. G. Cullum, 1967
Museum of Fine Arts, Museum of New Mexico, Santa Fe, NM

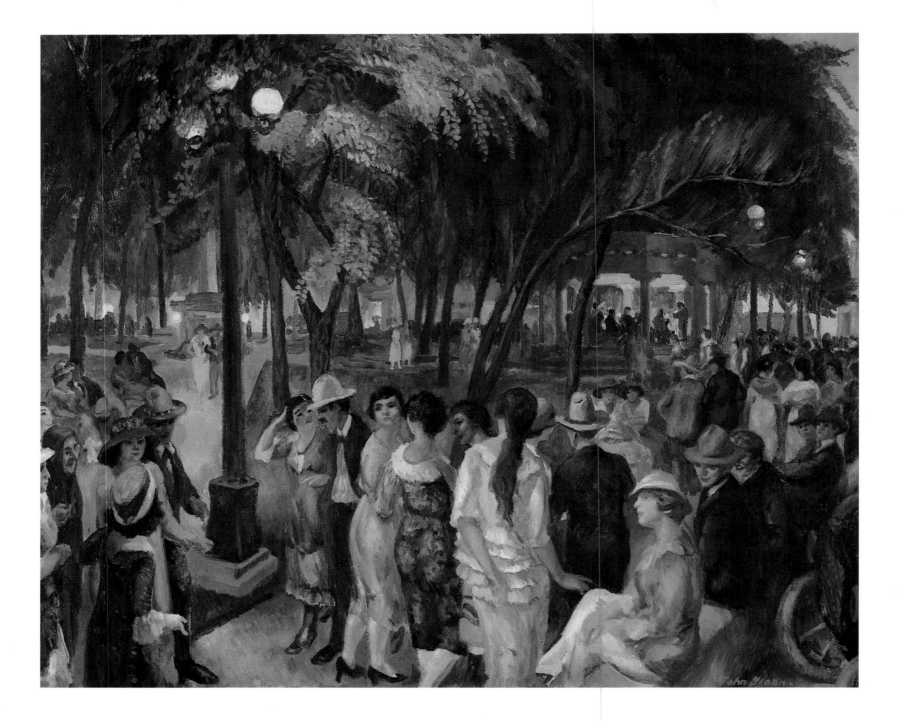

JOHN SLOAN (1871-1951)
The Plaza, Evening Santa Fe (Music in the Plaza)
1920, oil on canvas, 26 × 32 in.
Gift of Mrs. Cyrus McCormick, 1952
Museum of Fine Arts, Museum of New Mexico, Santa Fe, NM

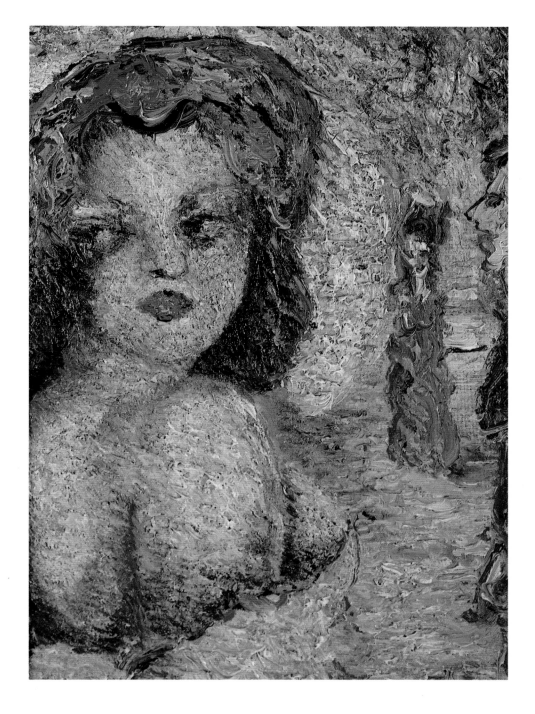

Alfred Morang (1902-1958)
Lady of the Evening
c. 1950, oil on canvas, 19 × 13 in.
Collection of Walt and Roynel Wiggins
Photo courtesy of the Cline Fine Art Gallery, Santa Fe, NM

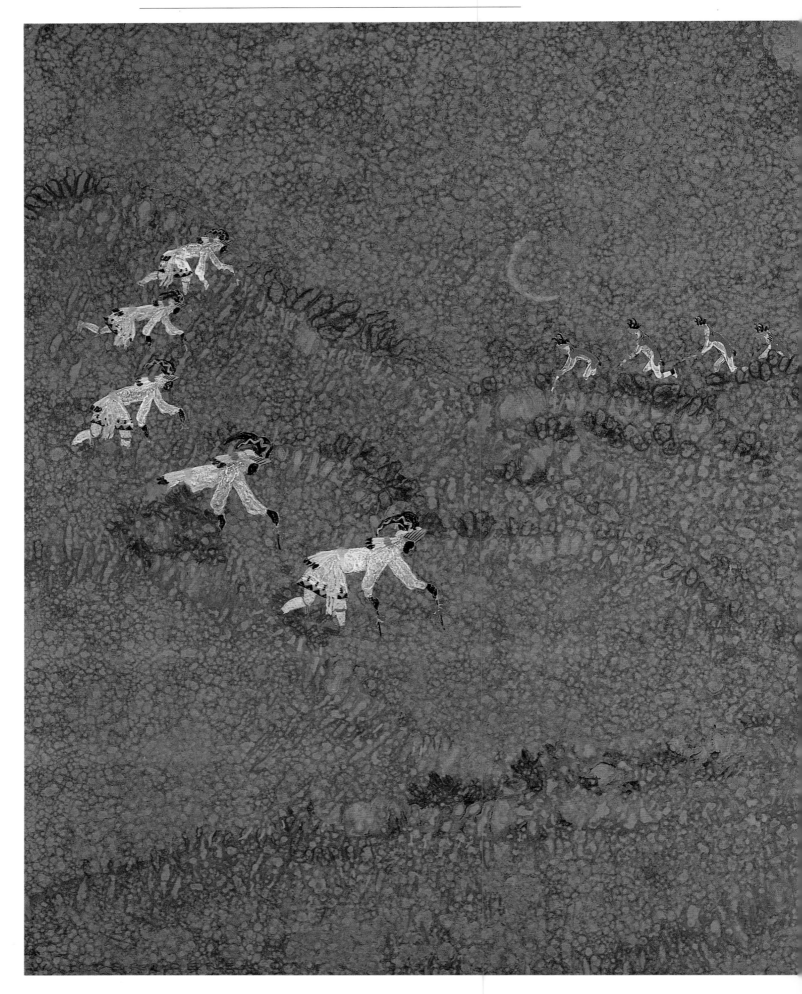

Gustave Baumann (1881-1971)
Winter Ceremony – Deer Dance
1922, oil on wood panel, 30½ × 52½ in.
Gift of Florence Dibele Bartlett, 1948
Museum of Fine Arts, Museum of New Mexico, Santa Fe, NM

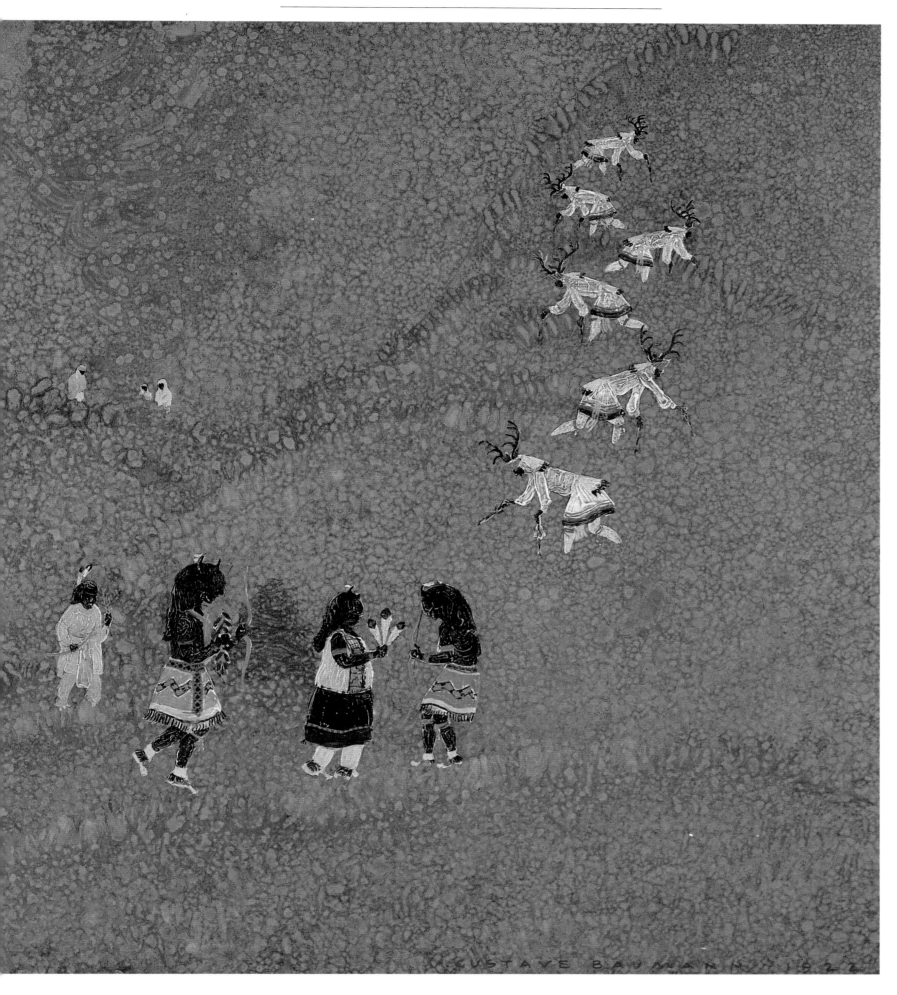

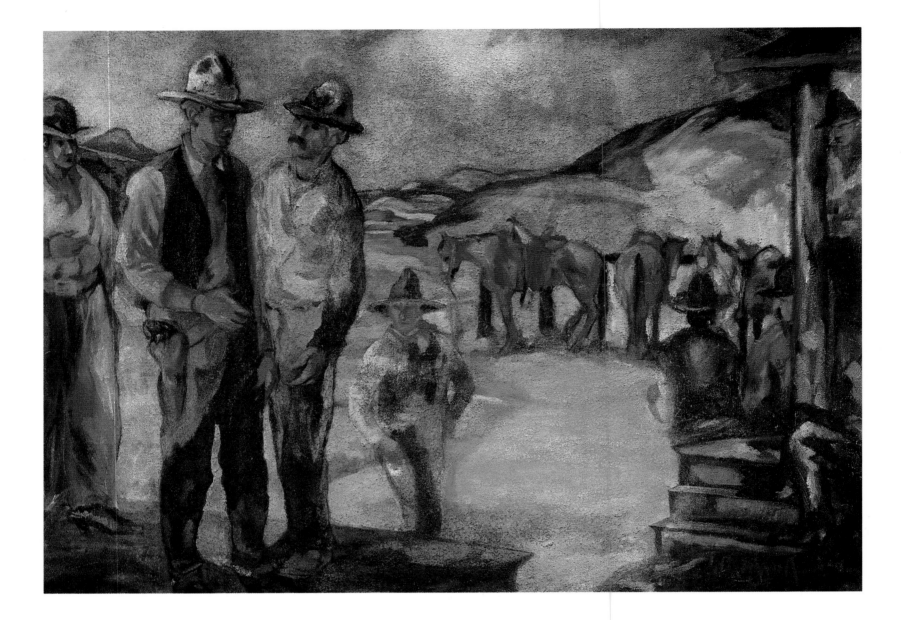

WALTER MRUK (1895-1942)
Border Town
n.d., oil on canvas, 21¼ × 29 in.
Photo courtesy of the Gerald Peters Gallery, Santa Fe, NM

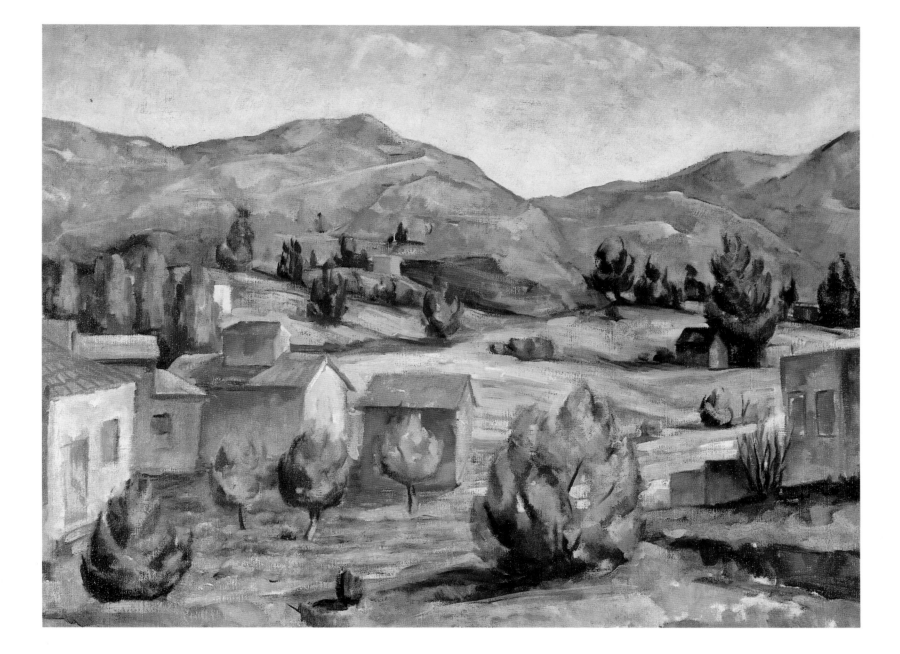

WILLARD NASH (1898-1943)
Santa Fe Landscape
n.d., oil on canvas, 30 × 40 in.
Courtesy of the Anschutz Collection, Denver, CO
Photo by James O. Milmoe

WILL SHUSTER (1893-1969)
Corn Dance
1920, oil on canvas, 26 × 37⅓ in.
Photo courtesy of the Gerald Peters Gallery, Santa Fe, NM

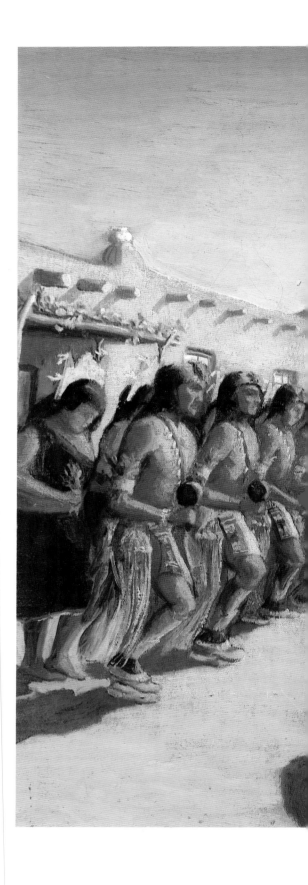

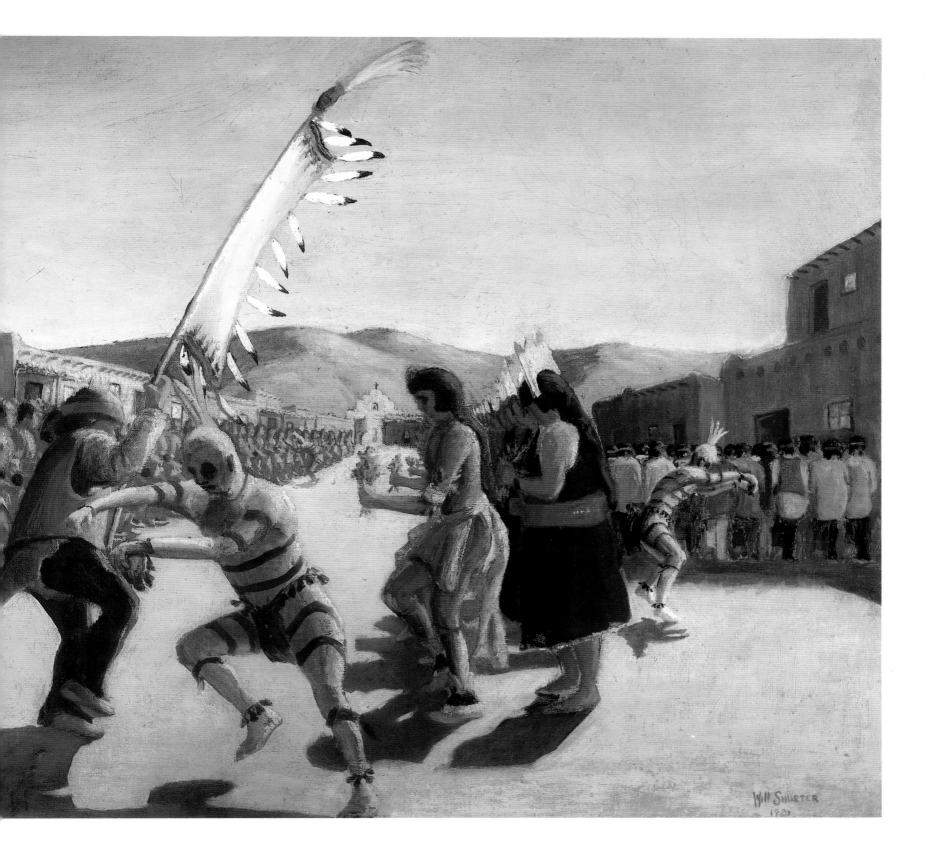

Overleaf:
FREMONT ELLIS (1897-1985)
Canyon de Chelly
n.d., watercolor, 21½ × 27¼ in.
Photo courtesy of the Gerald Peters Gallery, Santa Fe, NM

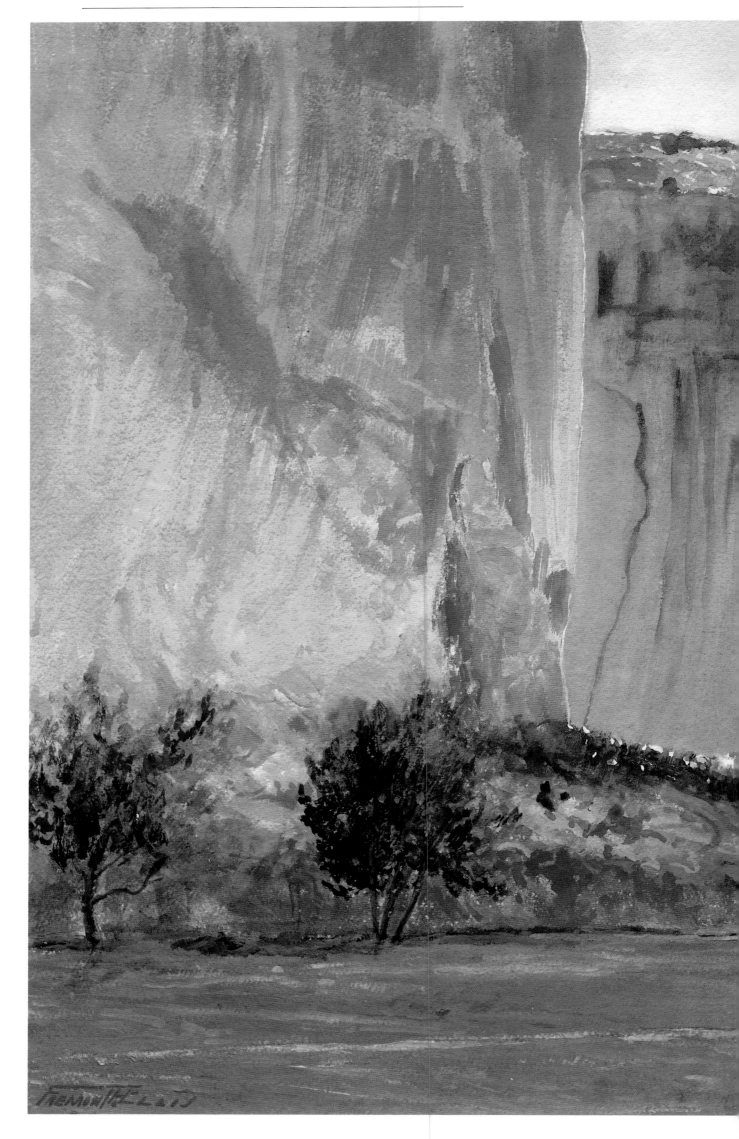

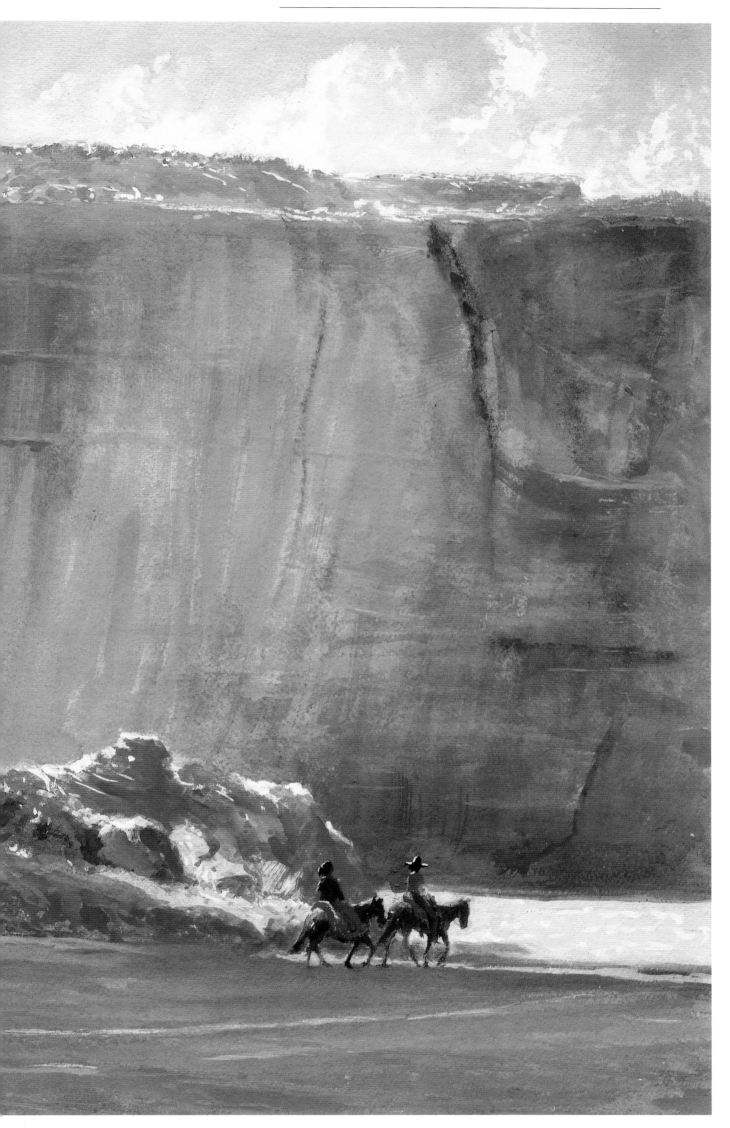

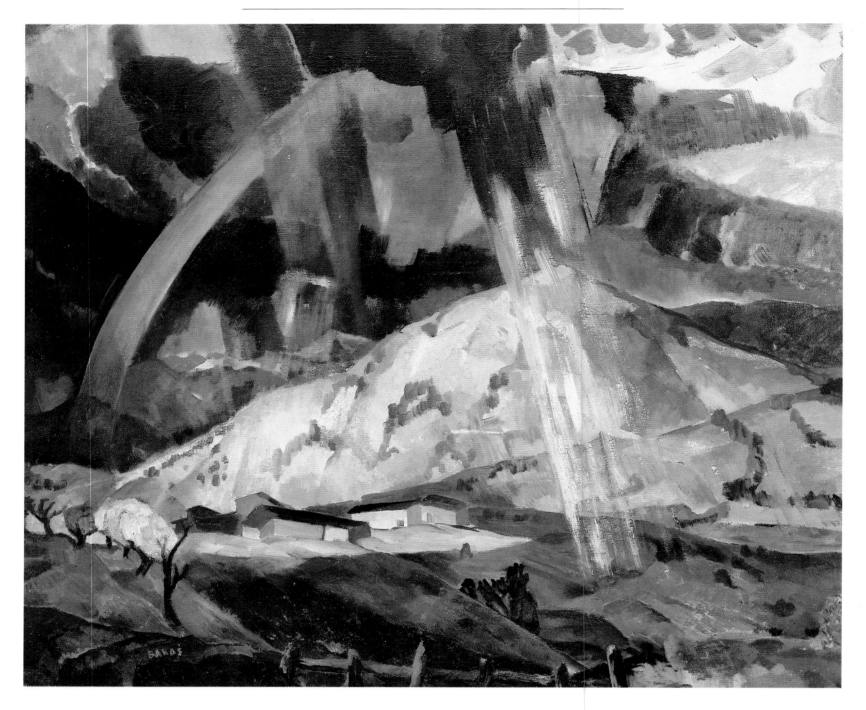

Józef Bakoś (1891-1977)
The Springtime Rainbow
1923, oil on canvas, 29½ × 35½ in.
Gift of the Artist in honor of Teresa Bakoś, 1974
Museum of Fine Arts, Museum of New Mexico, Santa Fe, NM

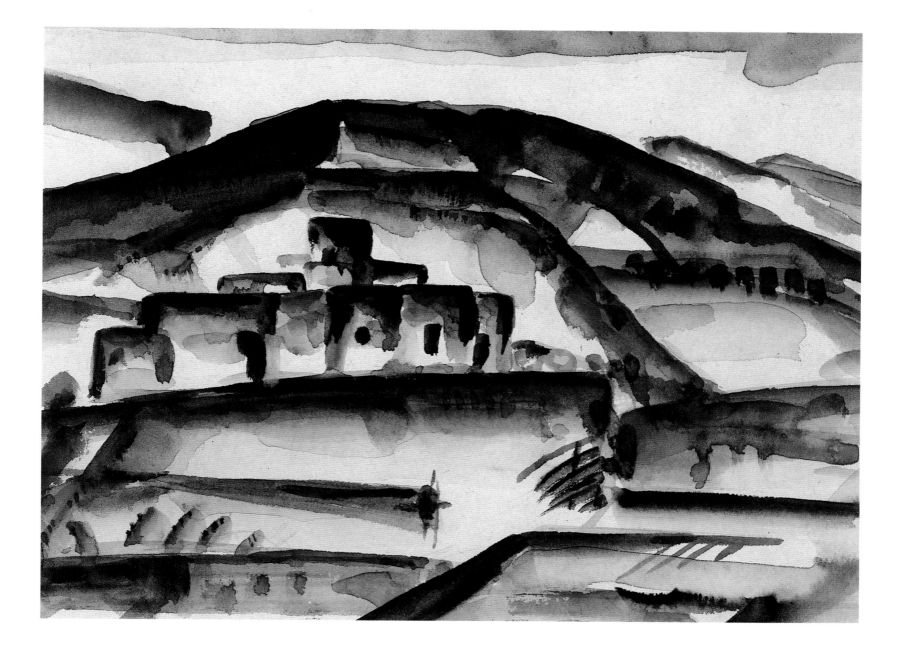

FRANK APPLEGATE (1882-1931)
Untitled – Village/Blue/Brown
n.d., watercolor, 6 × 8¾ in.
Photo courtesy of the Gerald Peters Gallery, Santa Fe, NM

O'KEEFFE, TRANSCENDENTALISM AND ABSTRACT ART

When Georgia O'Keeffe arrived on the train just south of Santa Fe with Rebecca Salsbury James in 1929, there were no flat tires or broken wagon wheels, but only the silent stainless-steel rails gleaming in the desert sun as witness to the beginning of another new era of New Mexican art.

As quiet in her person as her entry was to the bustling art colonies of Taos and Santa Fe, O'Keeffe immediately felt at home in the desert. Already an established, successful painter, O'Keeffe's highly personal, frontally patterned, harmoniously colored abstractions were selling in New York at her husband Alfred Stieglitz's avant-garde Gallery 291 in New York, where she had her first solo show in 1917.

O'Keeffe's love of the desert dated back to the four years between 1912 and 1918 that she spent teaching in Texas. While there, she spent most of her time alone exploring the desert. O'Keeffe would take off by herself (unheard of for a "lady" in those days) into the wilds, wearing men's black walking boots and carrying her art supplies, and spend entire days sketching and painting the uncharted desert-scapes before her.

Though she had studied at the Art Institute of Chicago and the Art Students League in New York, O'Keeffe insisted that she was influenced not by other people's work but by what she *saw* – in the landscape, architecture, gardens and found-object bones of New Mexico. In these passions O'Keeffe was not unlike many of the painters arriving in New Mexico at the same time. Perhaps because they were drawing from the same well, many of the Modernist, Abstract, and Transcendentalist painters produced images remarkably similar to O'Keeffe's. The receding mountains seen in O'Keeffe's *Black Cross, New Mexico* are echoed in the works of others that were painted both before and after O'Keeffe painted *Black Cross* in 1929. Such overlapping can be explained this way: The landscape in northern New Mexico is flooded with light that varies with an intensity that changes constantly as one gazes out toward the horizon, and whether a painter or not, one sees it. How one then chooses to represent such an image is up to the individual. All of the abstract painters were involved with reaching the essential shape, or in some cases, spirit, beneath what one actually *sees* on the horizon. O'Keeffe was a keen observer, as was her traveling partner, Rebecca Salsbury James, and the dialogue between the two is visible in their works of art.

Abstraction is a natural outcome of the desert. Marsden Hartley discovered this, as did the ancient ones of Chaco Canyon and other Anasazi cities who carved spirals and other abstract symbols in petroglyphs everywhere in the Southwest. Abstract painting occurred early in the twentieth century, in Santa Fe and Taos, and makes up a great portion of the art being made there today – much more than can be included in this history. Other major abstract painters working in the Southwest today include John Connell, Alan Graham, Reg Loving, Elmer Schooley, Rick Dillingham, Richard Tuttle, and Larry Bell, just to name a few.

The plates presented in this chapter represent nearly 70 years of abstract work by Santa Fe and Taos painters, some associated with the Transcendentalists and others not associated with any "school" or movement, who have chosen the Southwest as a place to work in isolation, or in tolerant coexistence with the Figurative, Landscape and Post-Modernist painters living there.

From O'Keeffe's highly recognizable works that explore shape, color and light via a Penitente cross, an adobe church, and a bleached skull and flowers; to Howard Cook's and Beatrice Mandelman's Cubist works (Mandelman, who studied with Léger in Paris, took Cubism farther than any other Southwestern painter next to Andrew Dasburg); to Tom Benrimo, the sole Surrealist of the group; to Doris Cross, originally an Abstract Expressionist who works with abstracted word "illuminations" much like twentieth-century William Blakes; and Agnes Martin, painter of spare and meditative canvases often incorporating linear elements, abstraction is expressed in extremely different styles in the Southwest.

Emil Bisttram and William Lumpkins, cornerstones of the Transcendentalist movement, approached painting as transformation, and took abstraction farther than any of their contemporaries. Similar to the Abstract Expressionists in some ways, the Transcendentalists emphasized "expression" in paint and took it into the realm of transformation.

Such contemporary abstract painters as Sam Scott, Eugene Newmann, Shelley Horton-Trippe and Emmi Whitehorse carry the Southwestern tradition of abstract painting past the Expressionists into a lyrical, transcendental realm that each transforms in paint, using the picture plane, light and color in a interaction that makes each of their interior landscapes unique and personal.

Jaune Quick-To-See Smith is a Native American Rauschenberg, utilizing found objects, photo-transfers and words, interacting with paint, to create an abstract kinetic surface that makes a statement as well as addresses painting.

Raymond Jonson, who with Bisttram founded the Transcendentalists, and John Marin, who painted in the Southwest from 1928 to 1930, were both masters of Modernist watercolor works. Jorge Fick, who was graduated from Black Mountain College in 1955 by Franz Kline, has painted in isolation outside of Santa Fe for nearly 30 years. Where Marin and Johnson fractured the picture plane to create light and color, Jorge Fick, more like Mondrian, uses color and geometric forms to energize the picture plane.

Abstract painting is alive and well in the Southwest. As Sam Scott eloquently puts it, "In the city the function of art is as an arbitrator of meaning that takes the place of Nature, but when you live in a light that is absolutely unique in the world, you are given an opportunity for a direct contact with the source . . . the experience of light as grace. . . . The nature of abstraction is recognition of simultaneous realities. . . . you are freed from narration and given the gift of beholding the mystery."

GEORGIA O'KEEFFE (1887-1986)
Black Cross, New Mexico
1929, oil on canvas, 39 × 30⅓ in.
The Art Institute Purchase Fund
The Art Institute of Chicago, IL

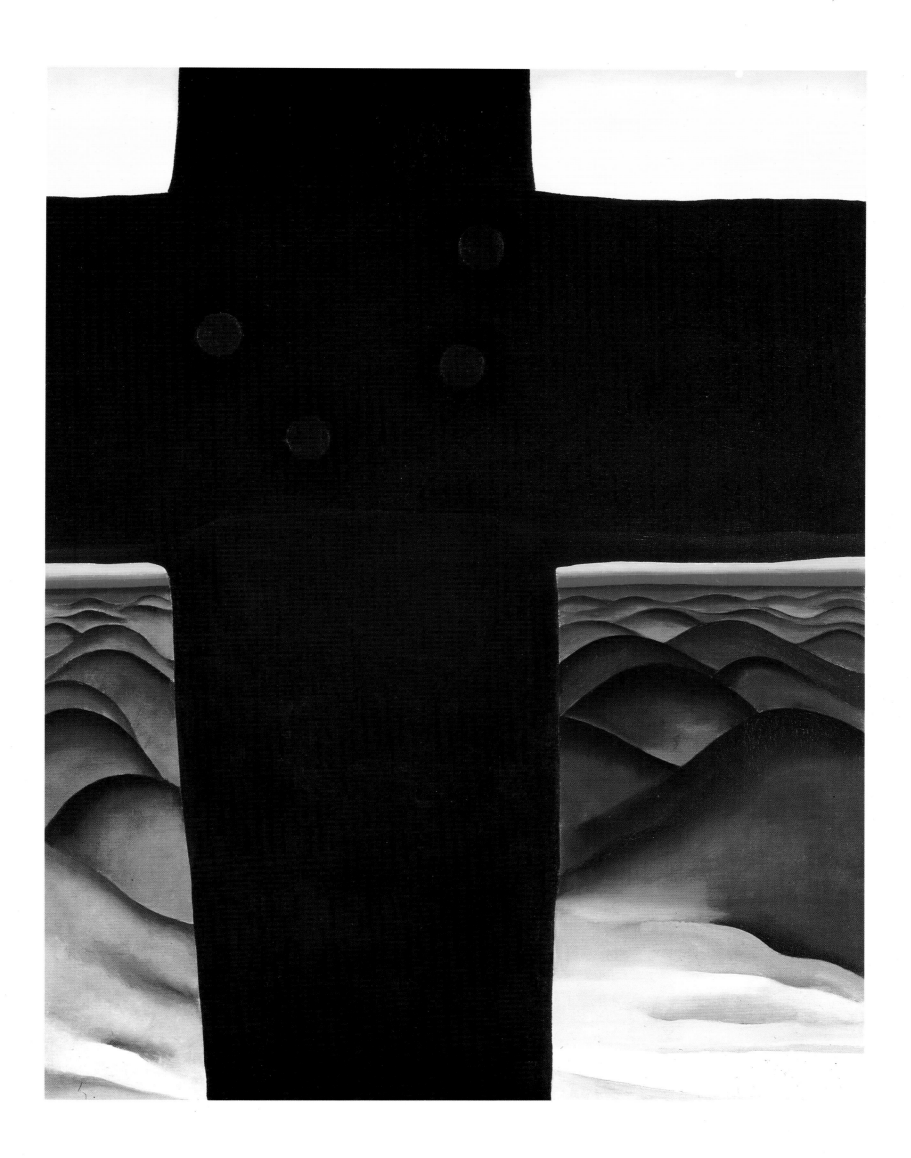

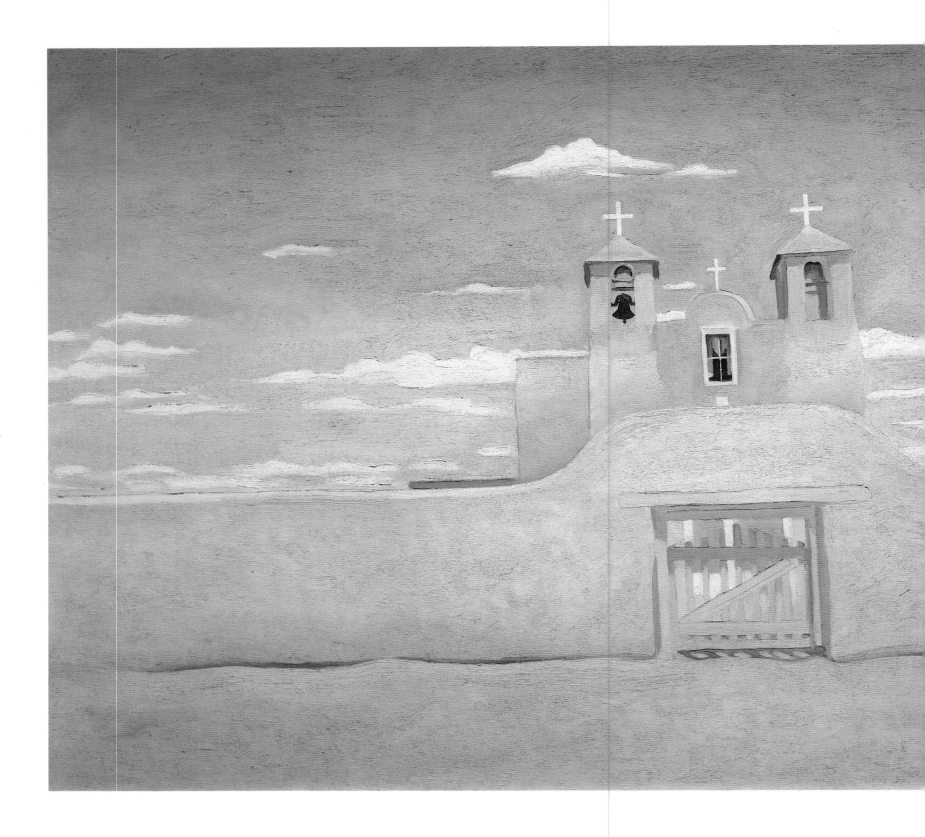

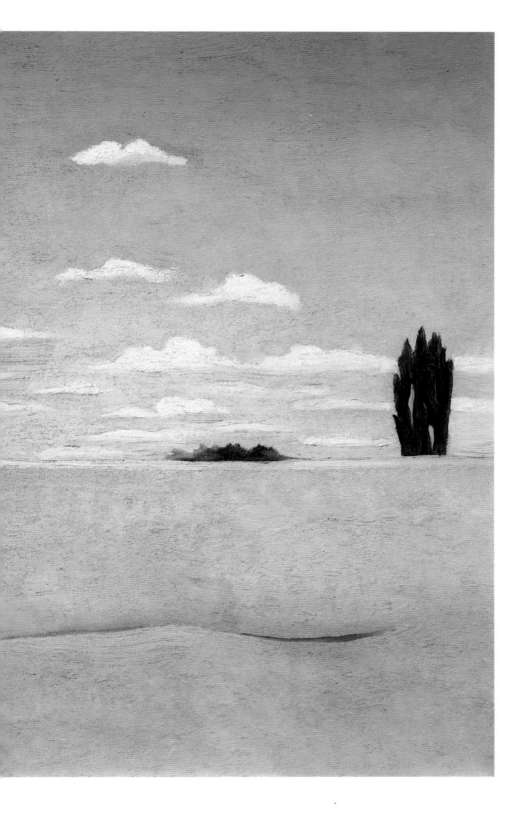

Georgia O'Keeffe
Front of Ranchos Church
1930, oil on canvas, 20 × 30 in.
Photo courtesy of the Gerald Peters Gallery, Santa Fe, NM

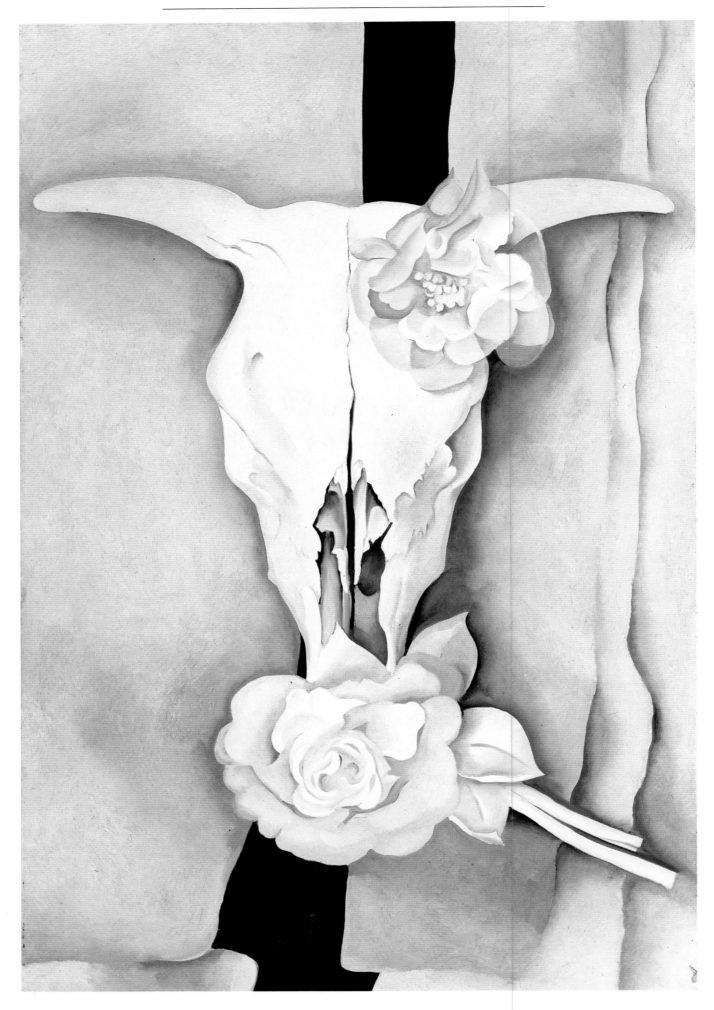

Georgia O'Keeffe
Skull with Calico Roses
1931, oil on canvas, 35$\frac{2}{3}$ × 24 in.
Gift of Georgia O'Keeffe, 1947
The Art Institute of Chicago, IL

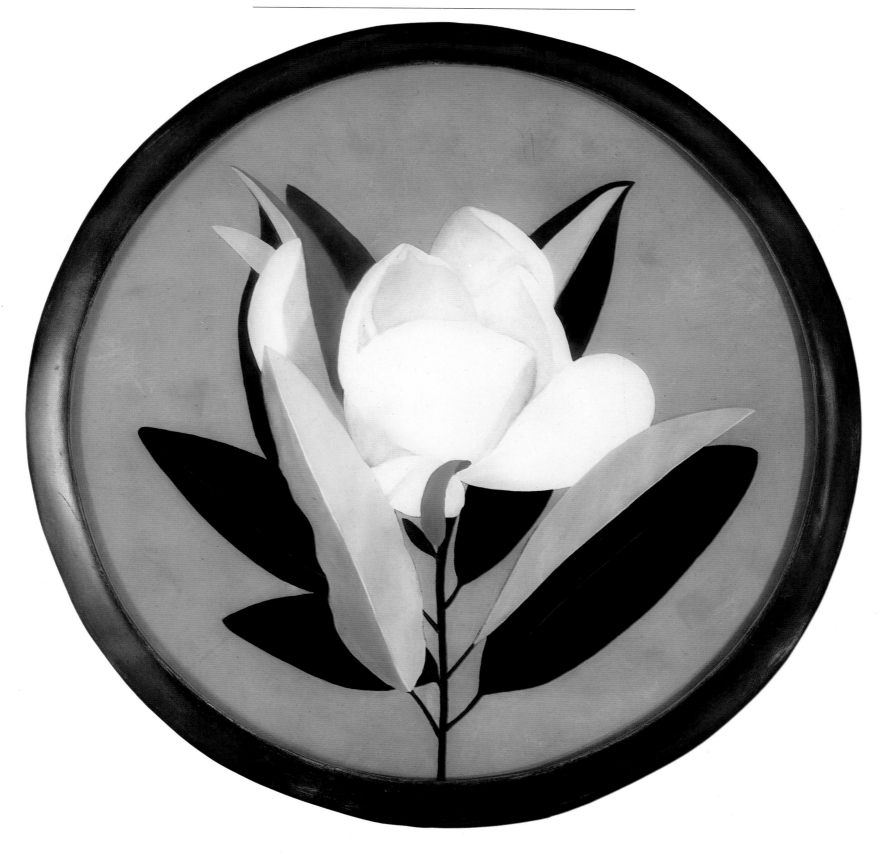

Rebecca Salsbury James (1891-1968)
Untitled (Magnolia)
n.d., oil on glass, 18¼ in. diameter
Photo courtesy of the Gerald Peters Gallery, Santa Fe, NM

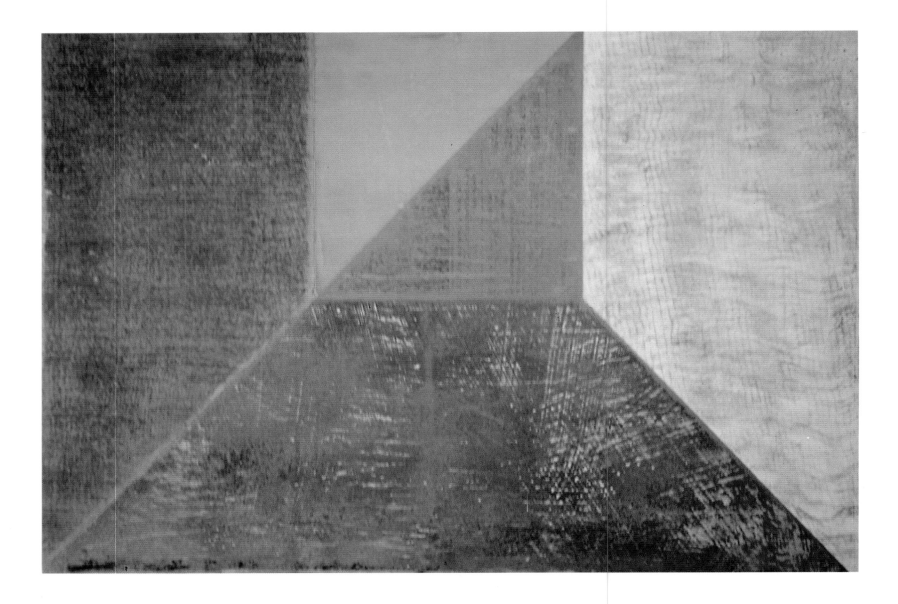

JORGE FICK (1932-   )
The Child's Room Window Was Open
1989, acrylic Plasti-kote on plywood, 11⅞ × 15¾ in.
Courtesy of the Artist

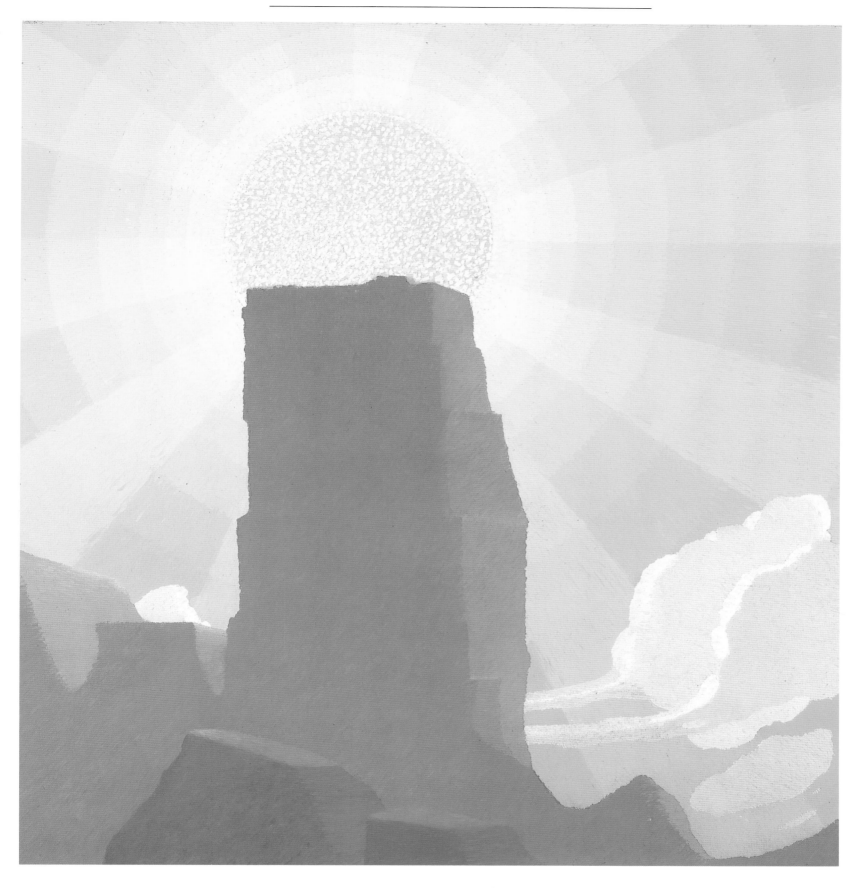

RAYMOND JONSON (1891-1982)
Light
1917, oil on canvas, 45 × 41½ in.
Gift of John Curtis Underwood, 1925
Museum of Fine Arts, Museum of New Mexico, Santa Fe, NM

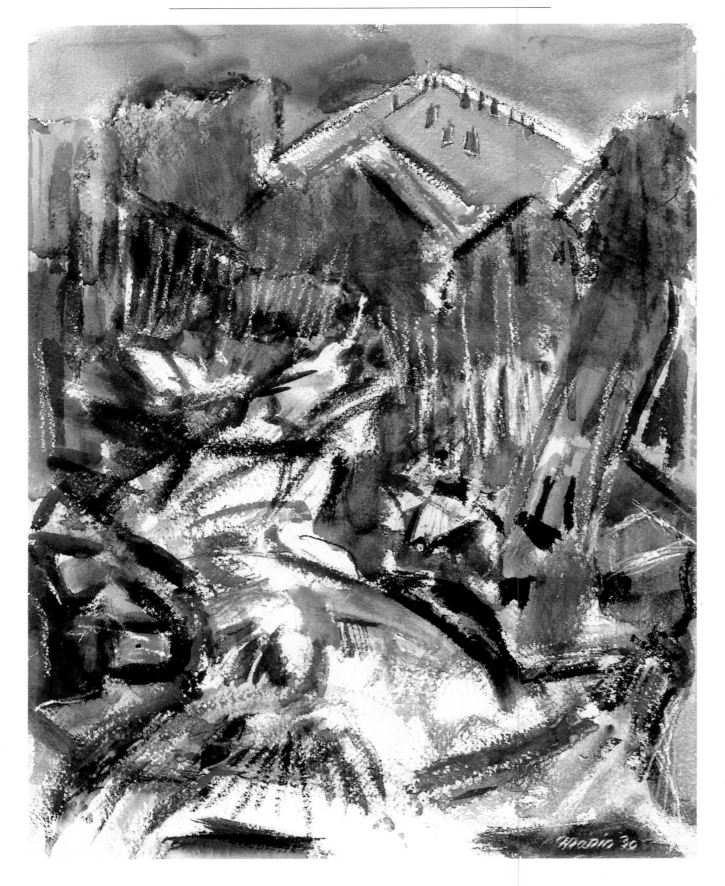

John Marin (1870-1953)
Blue Sky, Mountain Aspens, and the Roaring Hondo, NM
1930, watercolor, 19½ × 15½ in.
Courtesy of the Anschutz Collection, Denver, CO
Photo by James O. Milmoe

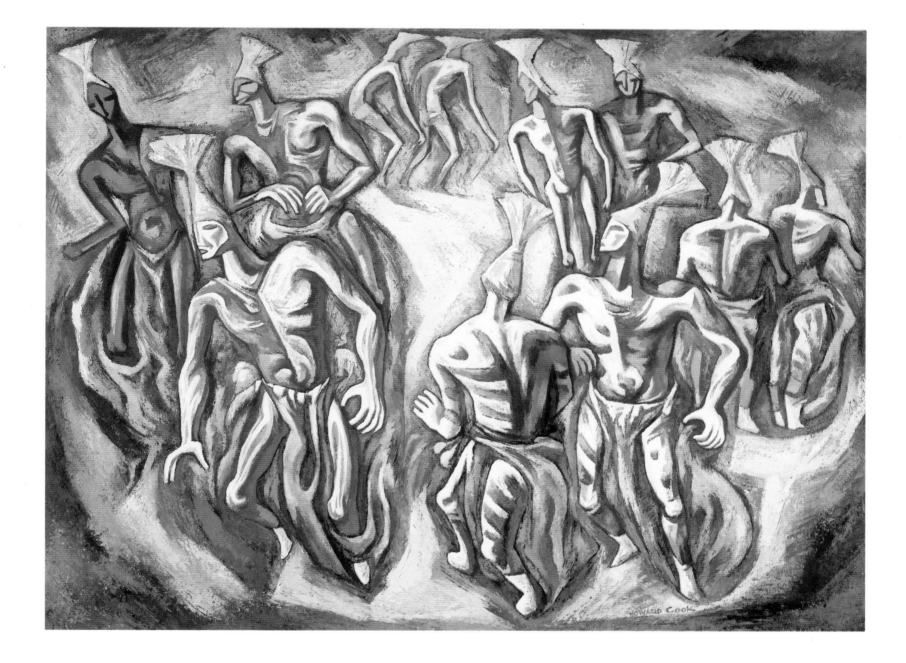

Howard Cook (1901-1980)
Koshare – Santo Domingo Corn Dance
1948, oil on canvas, 30 × 40 in.
Courtesy of the Anschutz Collection, Denver, CO
Photo by James O. Milmoe

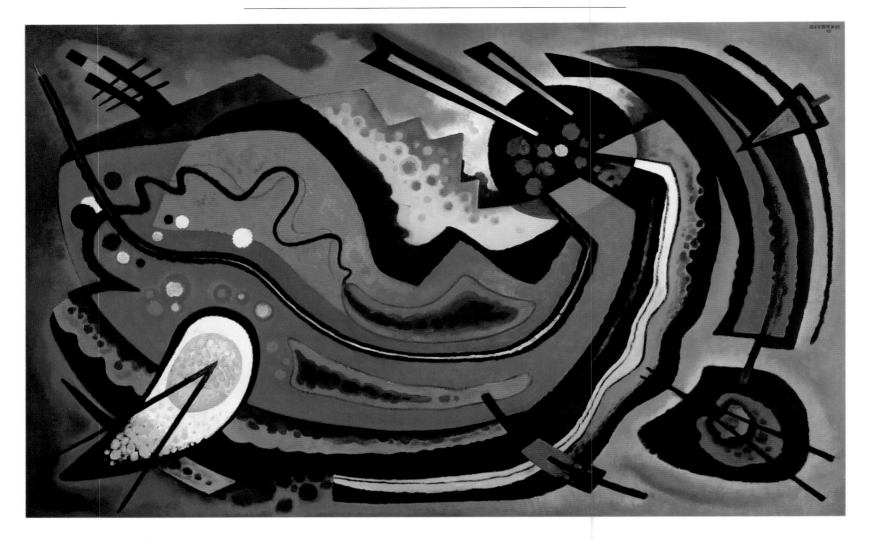

EMIL BISTTRAM (1895-1976)
Musical Notes
1951, acrylic on canvas, 50 × 80 in.
Collection of Walt and Roynel Wiggins
Photo courtesy of the Cline Fine Art Gallery, Santa Fe, NM

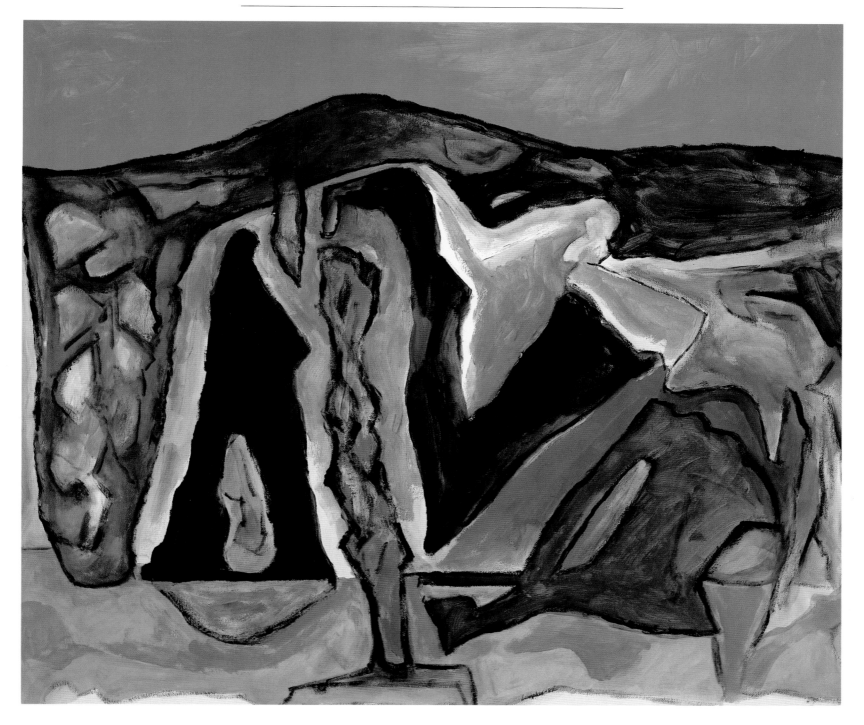

WILLIAM LUMPKINS (1909-   )
New Mexico Landscape
1987, acrylic, 43 × 51½ in.
Collection of Walt and Roynel Wiggins
Photo courtesy of the Cline Fine Art Gallery, Santa Fe, NM

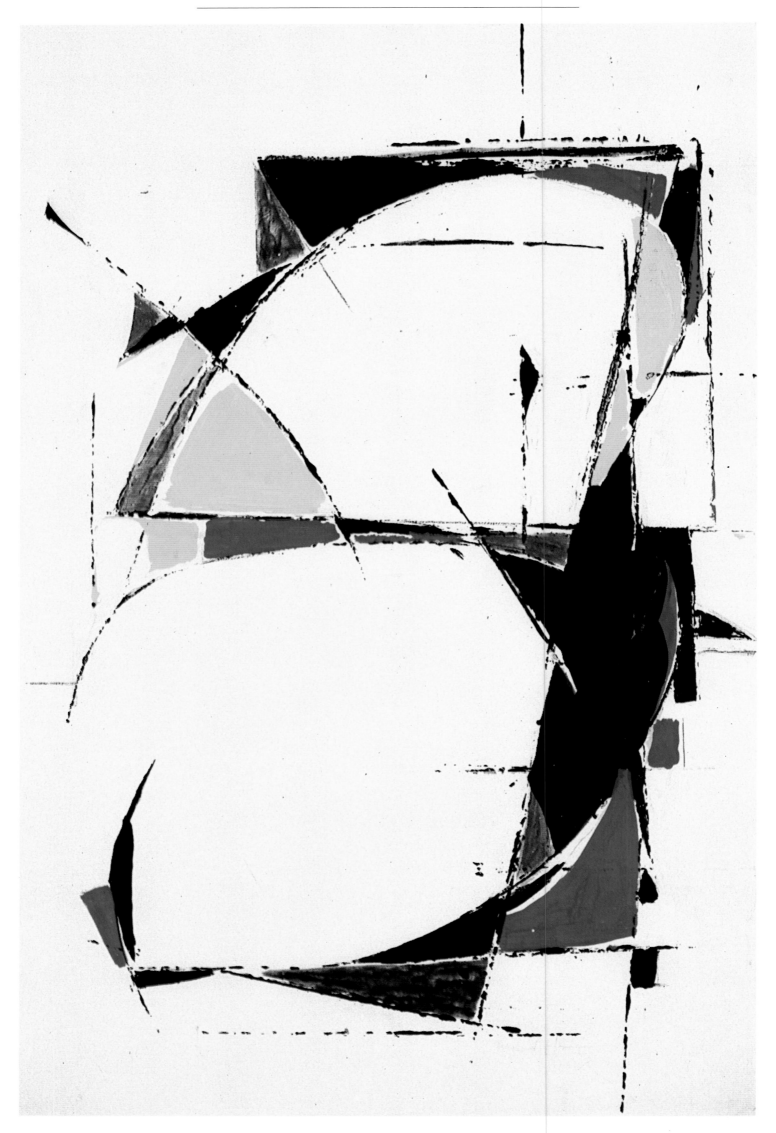

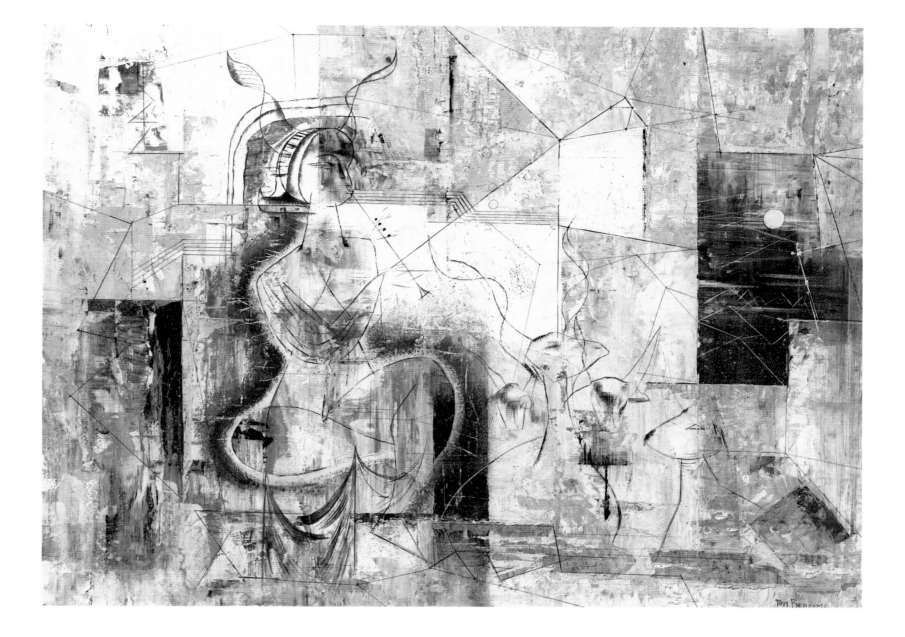

Left:

Beatrice Mandelman (1912-   )
White Time
1982, acrylic on canvas, 29½ × 19¾ in.
Collection of the Harwood Foundation, Taos, NM

Tom Benrimo (1887-1958)
Revelry in Space
c. 1951, casein on board, 14½ × 19¾ in.
Photo courtesy of the Mission Gallery, Taos, NM

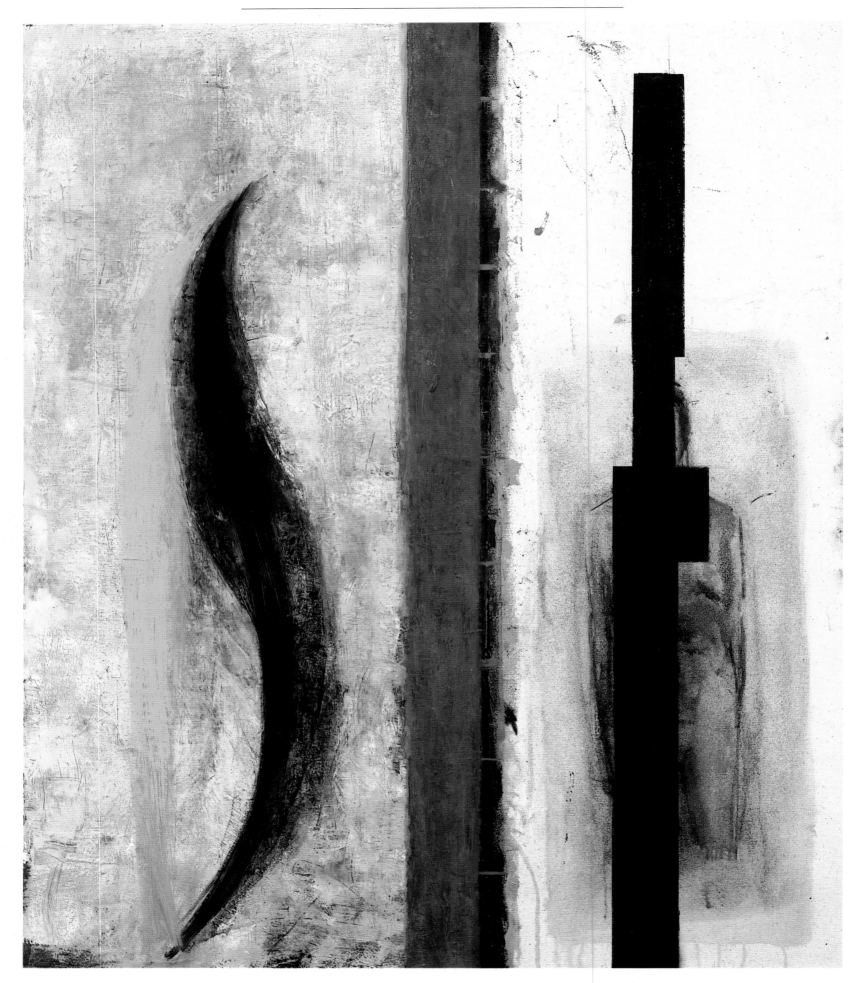

EUGENE NEWMANN (1936-   )
Figure and Sequel
1989, oil on canvas, 48 × 36 in.
Photo courtesy of the Linda Durham Gallery, Santa Fe, NM

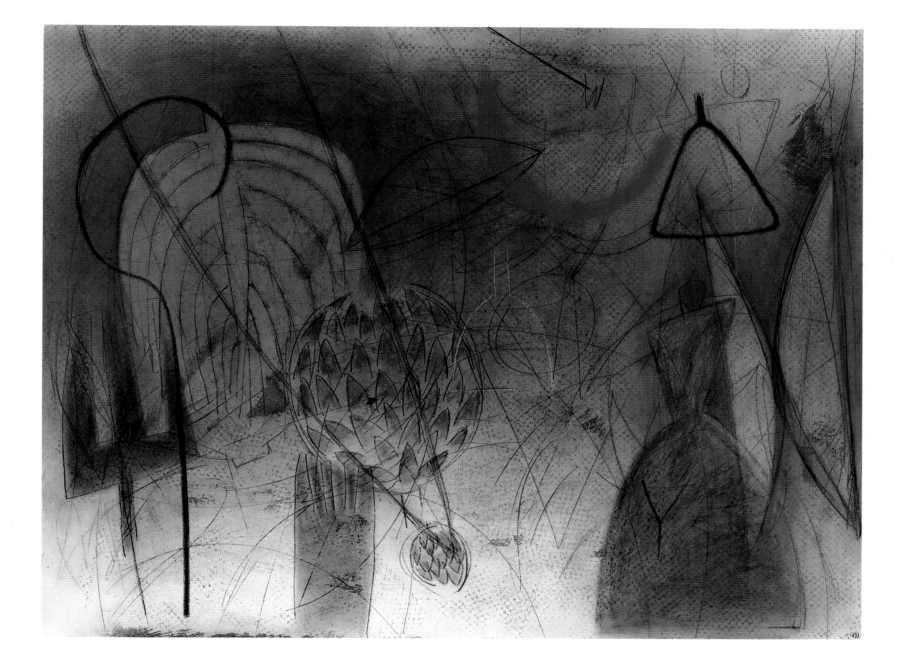

Emmi Whitehorse – Navajo (1956-   )
Fallen Seed
1990, oil and pastel on canvas, 39 × 51 in.
Private Collection
Photo courtesy of the LewAllen Gallery, Santa Fe, NM

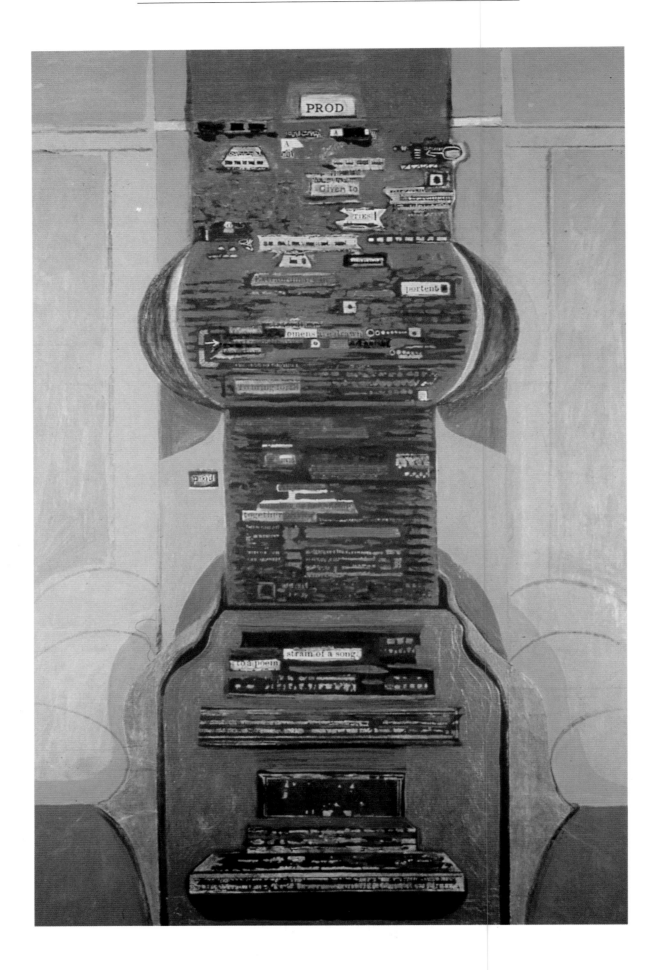

Doris Cross (1907-   )
Totem
1978, ink, acrylic, print and paper, 30 × 20 in.
Courtesy of Guy Cross

Agnes Martin (1914-   )
Untitled # 6
1980, acrylic and graphite on canvas, 72 × 72 in.
Gift of the American Art Foundation, 1982
Museum of Fine Arts, Museum of New Mexico, Santa Fe, NM

JAUNE QUICK-TO-SEE SMITH – SALISH (1940-   )
Oh! Zone
1992, mixed media/recycled material, 48 × 60 in.
Photo courtesy of the LewAllen Gallery, Santa Fe, NM

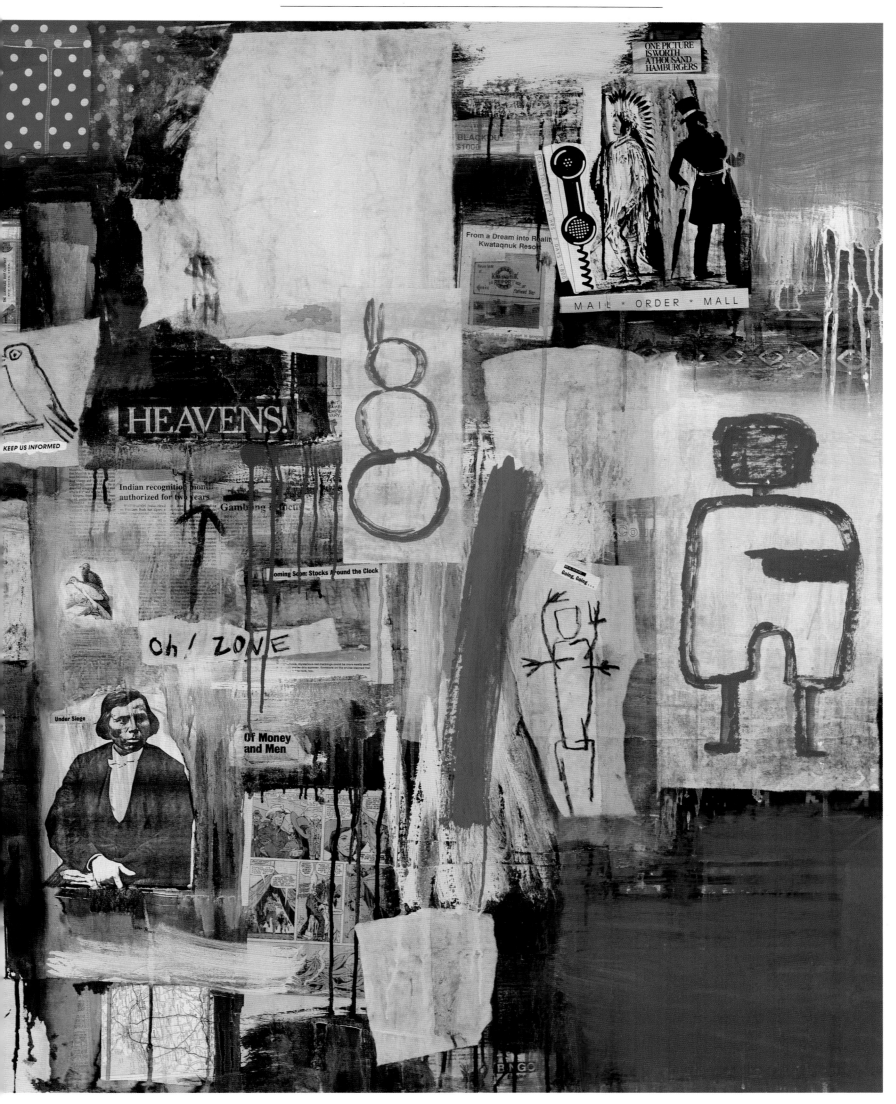

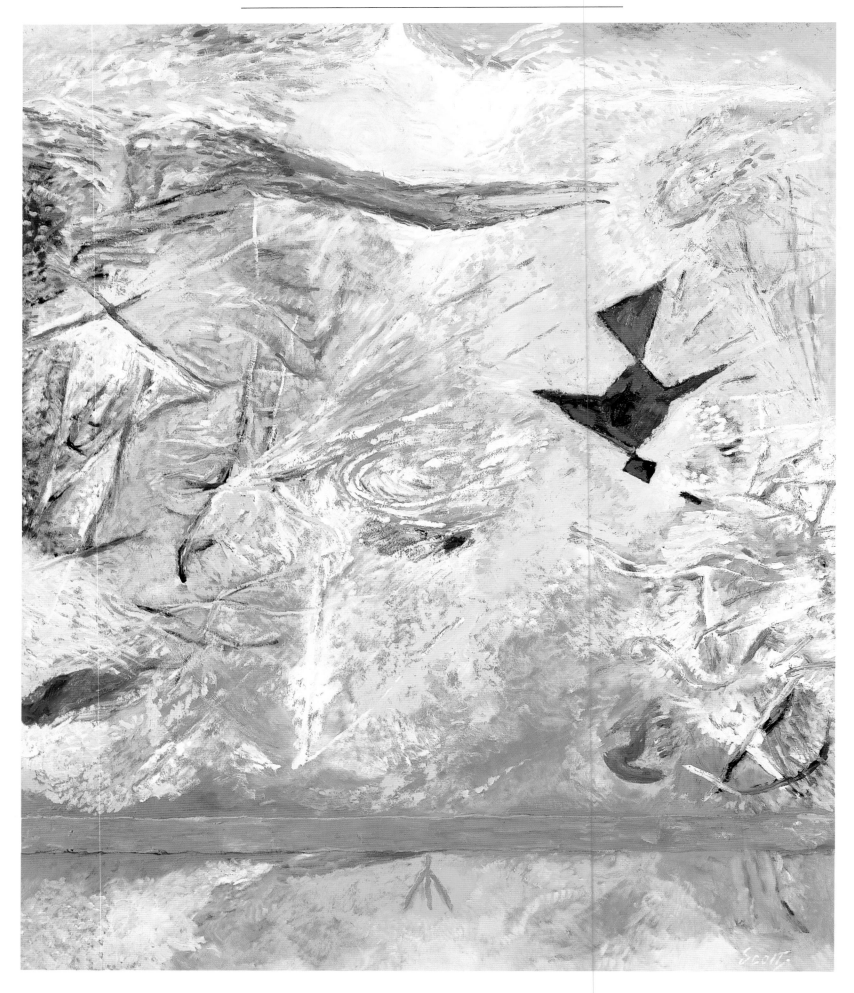

SAM SCOTT (1940-)
Rim
1987, oil on canvas, 80 × 66 in.
Donation of Kathleen Peters to the Santa Fe Art Foundation

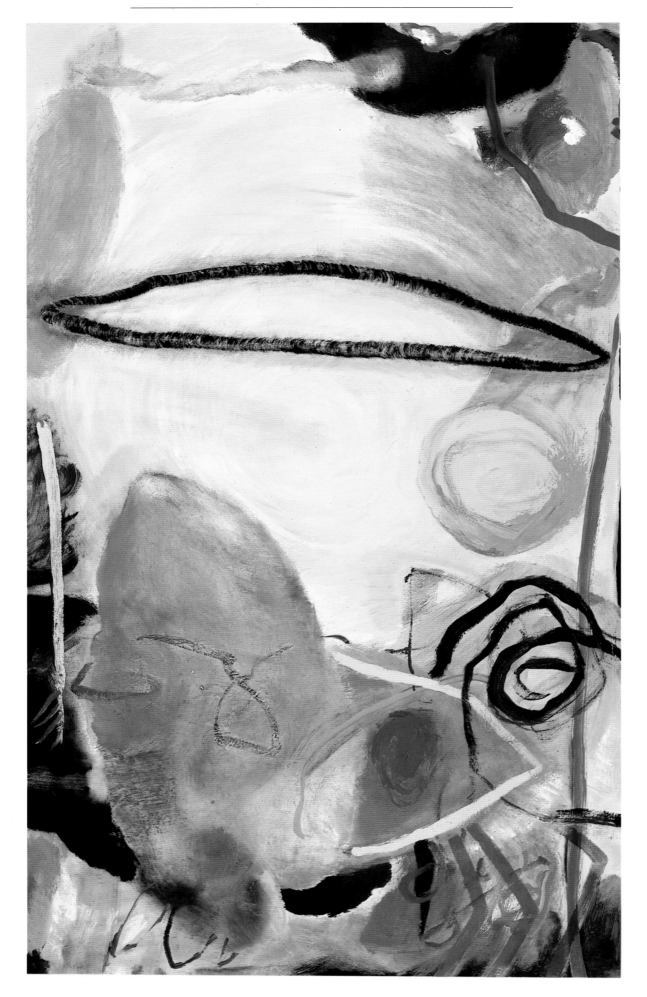

SHELLEY HORTON-TRIPPE (1951-   )
The Hunter
1991, oil on canvas, 72 × 44 in.
Private collection of Kathleen Peters

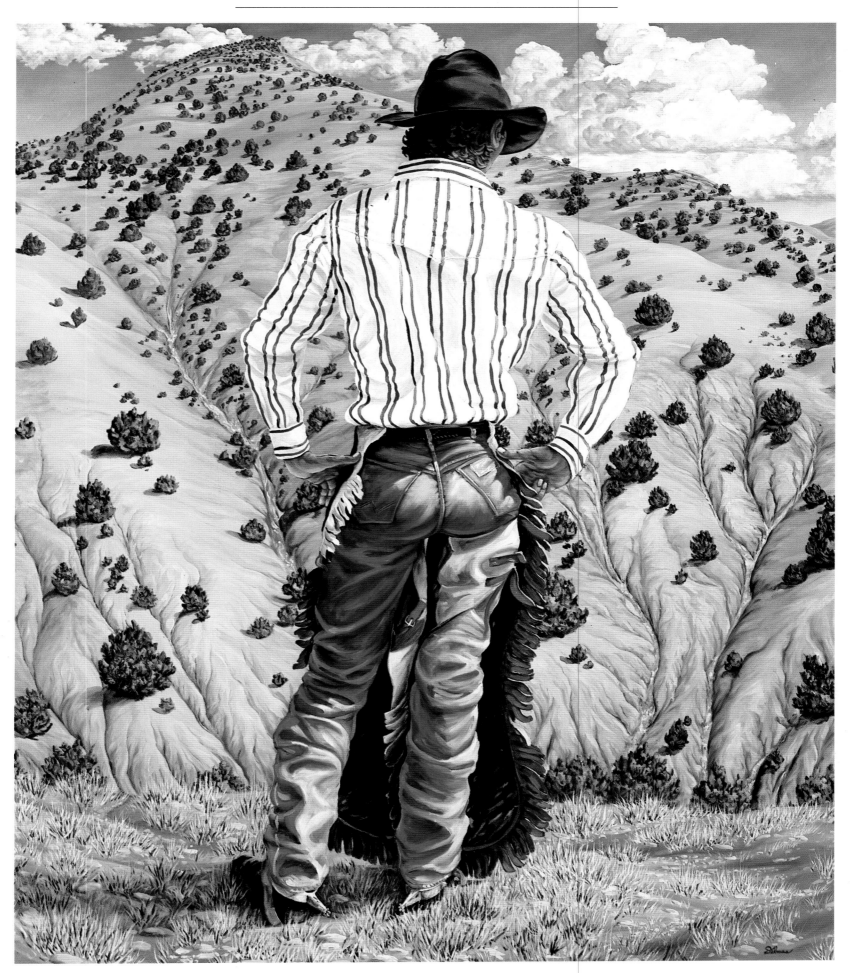

Delmas Howe (1935-)
Apollo's Half Acre
1991, oil on canvas, 68 × 59 in.
Photo courtesy of Copeland-Rutherford Fine Arts, Ltd.,
   Santa Fe, NM

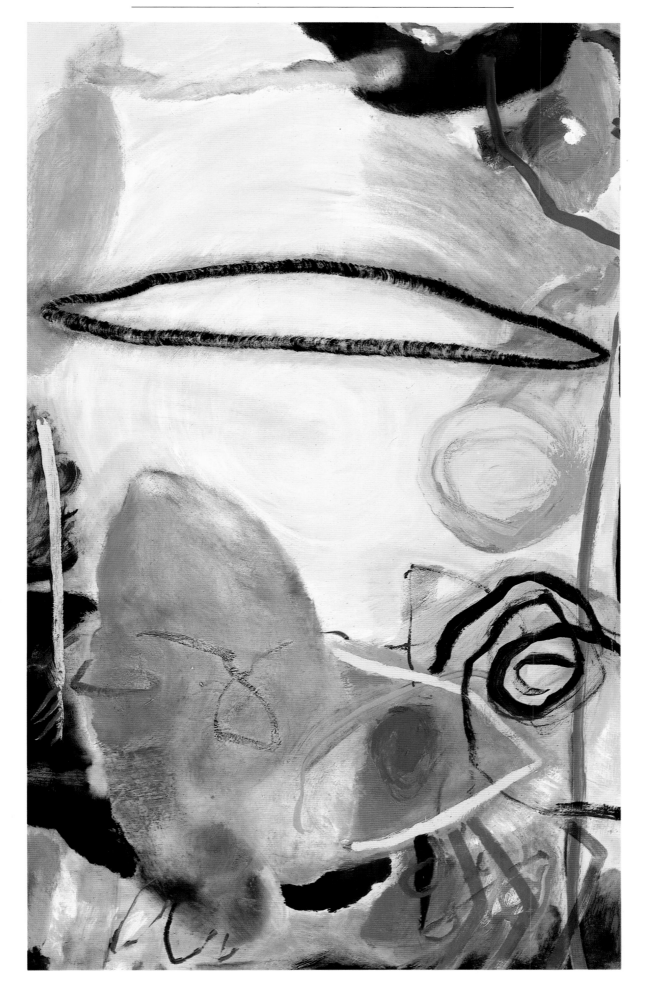

SHELLEY HORTON-TRIPPE (1951-   )
The Hunter
1991, oil on canvas, 72 × 44 in.
Private collection of Kathleen Peters

Contemporary Santa Fe and Taos Art

The fabled "light" of the Southwest, originally a metaphor for the gold of the Seven Cities that the Spaniards had been searching for, was to take on a exponentially larger and more destructive meaning when, in the 1940s, the secret Manhattan Project in Los Alamos, guided by Robert Oppenheimer, created a "light" that had the potential to destroy the face of the earth. The discovery and perfection of the nuclear age's weapons began and continues to this day at Los Alamos, a non-adobe city situated atop a mesa just slightly west of and almost directly between Taos and Santa Fe.

At least partially in response to this, many of today's Southwestern artists, including Luis Jimenez, Zara Kriegstein and Terry Allen (though certainly no one would group them into what could be called a "school") have, via their own styles, concentrated much of their work on socially conscious content, using words, visual metaphors, constructs, light, and shadow to create works that are as much about content as they are about medium. At the same time, each artist is dealing with the picture plane in a purely contemporary way.

Kathleen Morris's work relates to the archetypical realm much like that of symbolist Mary Greene Blumenschein, even though Morris, who paints in isolation as O'Keeffe did, has not been influenced by Mary Greene's work.

Ron Cooper is the Marcel Duchamp of the Southwest, working in many, seemingly disjunctive mediums, answering in his images what he describes as "questions" that arise through his work, hence moving in a visual continuum.

Delmas Howe is a modern-day W. Herbert Dunton, concentrating on portraits of cowboy life. Howe, however, takes his work a late-twentieth-century step further by conceptualizing his cowboys as a pantheon of the ancient gods, thus creating metaphor in paint.

Mark Spencer, who paints in extremely rare, classic Renaissance style, also creates metaphors in paint. His canvases radiate light even when the surface is pitch black.

Maurice Burns, Eli Levin, and Elias Rivera specialize, each in his own way, in painting genre scenes, sometimes depicting night life as did Alfred Morang, and other times producing tableaus of daily life in Santa Fe. Each of these painters is a master of light and oil paint, though their subjects are quite diverse.

Bernadette Vigil paints scenes depicting the religious life of the Hispanic culture using the soft lines and brilliant colors of the Mexican muralists, and an omniscient view that creates a supernatural perspective.

Carol Hoy uses the color theories of Abstract Expressionism combined with a background in Chinese brush stroke to create her own trademark abstracted images that vibrate with color and light.

Margaret Nes is a Taos artist who uses pastels and paint to create soft architectural images that use light to bend the shape of the buildings, giving the illusion of seeing the world through a convex lens. Her luminous works resemble the architectural work of Georgia O'Keeffe, but retain their individuality through the use of late-twentieth-century materials.

Douglas Johnson creates postcard-sized casein works on paper that are like tiny Diego Riveras. They reconstruct his vision of the Anasazi pueblos, often with a ritualistic content, while featuring realistically rendered birds and flowers in the foreground.

Many of the works of art depicted in this chapter were created by Native Americans, all of whom are alumni or faculty of, or affiliated with, the Institute of American Indian Arts (IAIA) in Santa Fe. The IAIA grew out of a studio school established in 1932 by Dorothy Dunn, a graduate of the Art Institute of Chicago and friend of many of the early painters. The Studio was located on the campus of the Santa Fe Indian School, a boarding school for tribal children. The Studio's focus was on introducing modern techniques of painting to Native American artists. In the early days, Gustave Baumann and John Sloan were actively involved in the school and its exhibitions. In the early 1930s, Sloan staged the largest show of Native American art ever assembled, in New York's Grand Central Palace Gallery, filling seven rooms with work representing 30 tribes of Native American artists.

The Studio, which included Allan Houser as one of the first Native Americans on the faculty, has been the foundation for 60 years of art-making and aesthetic exploration by Native Americans. It allowed them to begin to escape the pigeonholing associated with American Indian art forms, and to leap into the realm of the Modern. In 1961 The Studio officially became a part of the Institute of American Indian Arts, which is to this day the most vital indigenous art school in North America.

Not surprisingly, Emmi Whitehorse, Jaune Quick-To-See Smith (both of whose works can be seen in Chapter Three), Earl Biss, T. C. Cannon, Mateo Romero, Darren Vigil Gray, Fritz Scholder, R. C. Gorman and Allan Houser all were directly associated or affiliated with IAIA at one time or another. Maurice Burns, one of the few Afro-Americans painting in the Southwest, was also on the faculty at IAIA.

Though many of these painters gathered initial knowledge from IAIA, they also went on to study at other art schools and to achieve national recognition. Earl Biss received a degree from the San Francisco Art Institute, and Fritz Scholder received his MFA from the University of Arizona, as well as several honorary doctorates including one from the Salon D'Automne in Paris. T. C. Cannon, who died, tragically, at age 31, was featured in a two-man show with Fritz Scholder at the Smithsonian Institution when he was only 22.

Today, Native American artists are fulfilling the indigenous vision for themselves, drawing upon all of art history and revitalizing what the early Southwestern Anglo painters began, carrying Native American art far into the future.

Fritz Scholder – Southern Californian Mission (1937-   )
An American Portrait
1979, oil on canvas, 40 × 35 in.
Courtesy of the Anschutz Collection, Denver, CO
Photo by James O. Milmoe

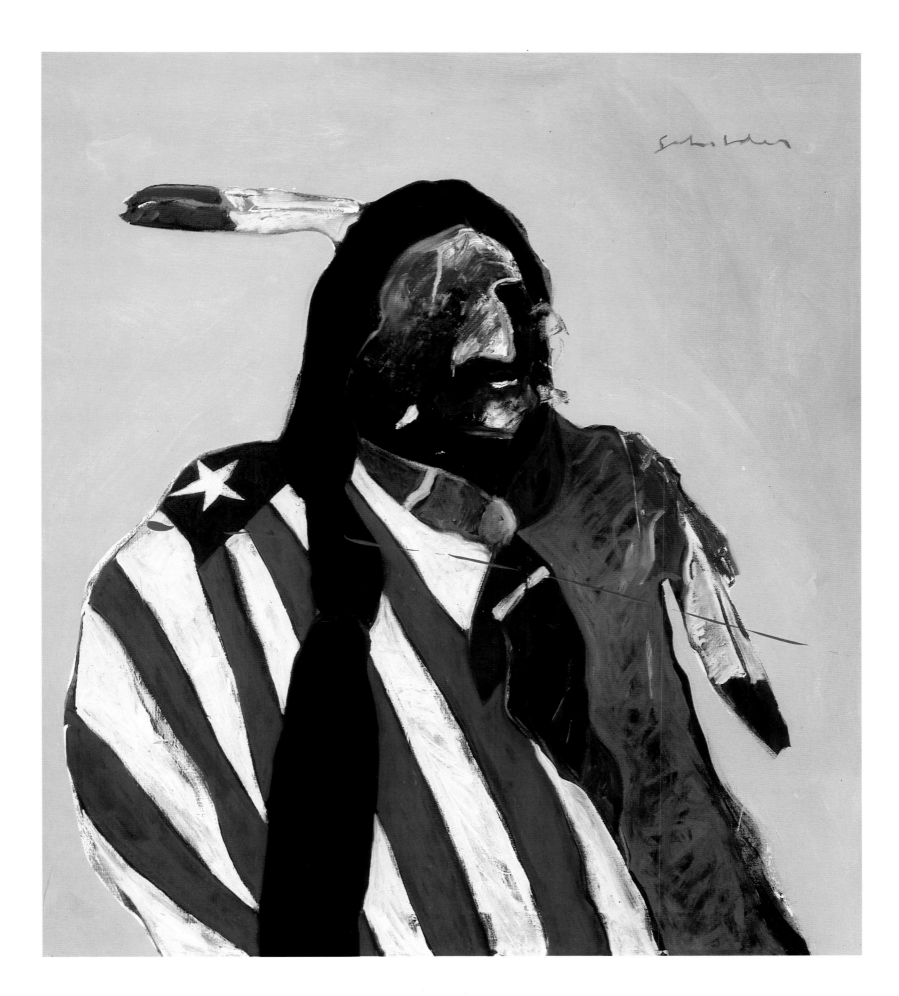

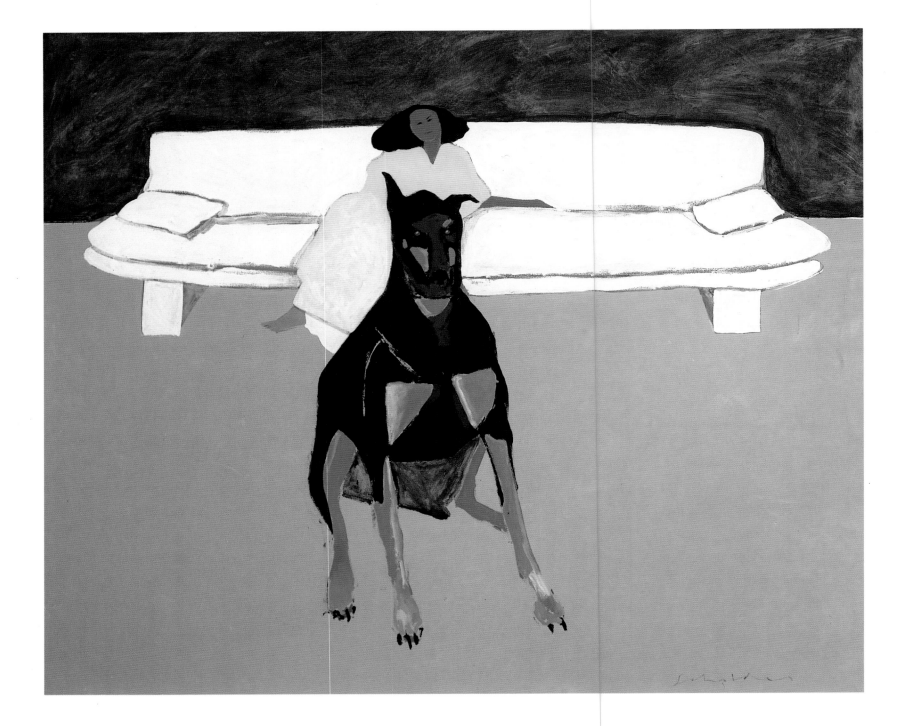

Fritz Scholder
Woman and Dog # 1
1992, acrylic on canvas, 68 × 80 in.
Photo courtesy of the Riva Yares Gallery, Scottsdale, AZ

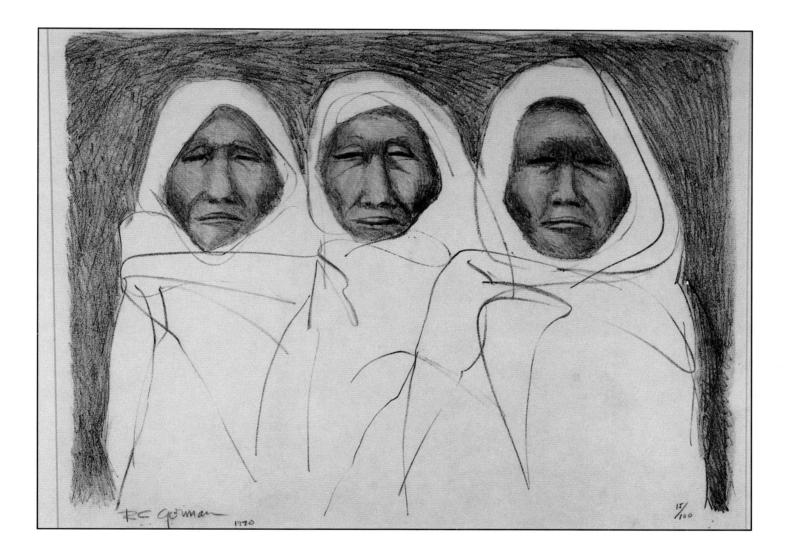

R. C. GORMAN – NAVAJO (1932-   )
Three Taos Men
1970, charcoal drawing, 19½ × 24 in.
Permanent collection of the Institute of American Indian Arts
   Museum, Santa Fe, NM
Photo by Larry Phillips

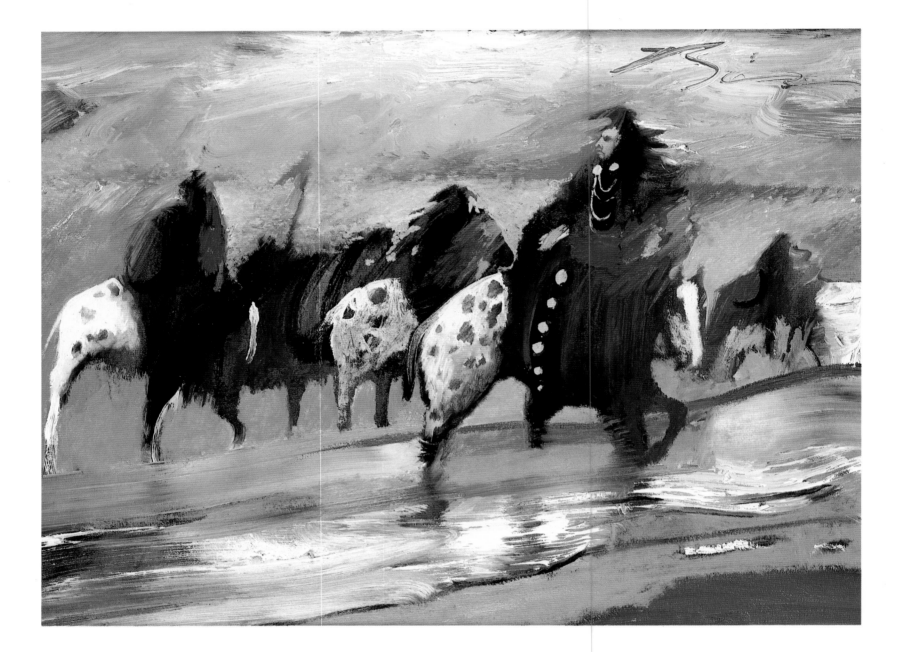

Earl Biss – Crow (1947-)
Retreating Through the Back Waters
1992, oil on canvas, 18 × 24 in.
Collection of the Artist
Photo courtesy of Joyner Publications, Ltd.

Right:
T. C. Cannon – Kiowa/Caddo (1947-1978)
Collector # 5
1975, oil and acrylic on canvas, 80 × 72 in.
Collection of Richard and Nancy Bloch

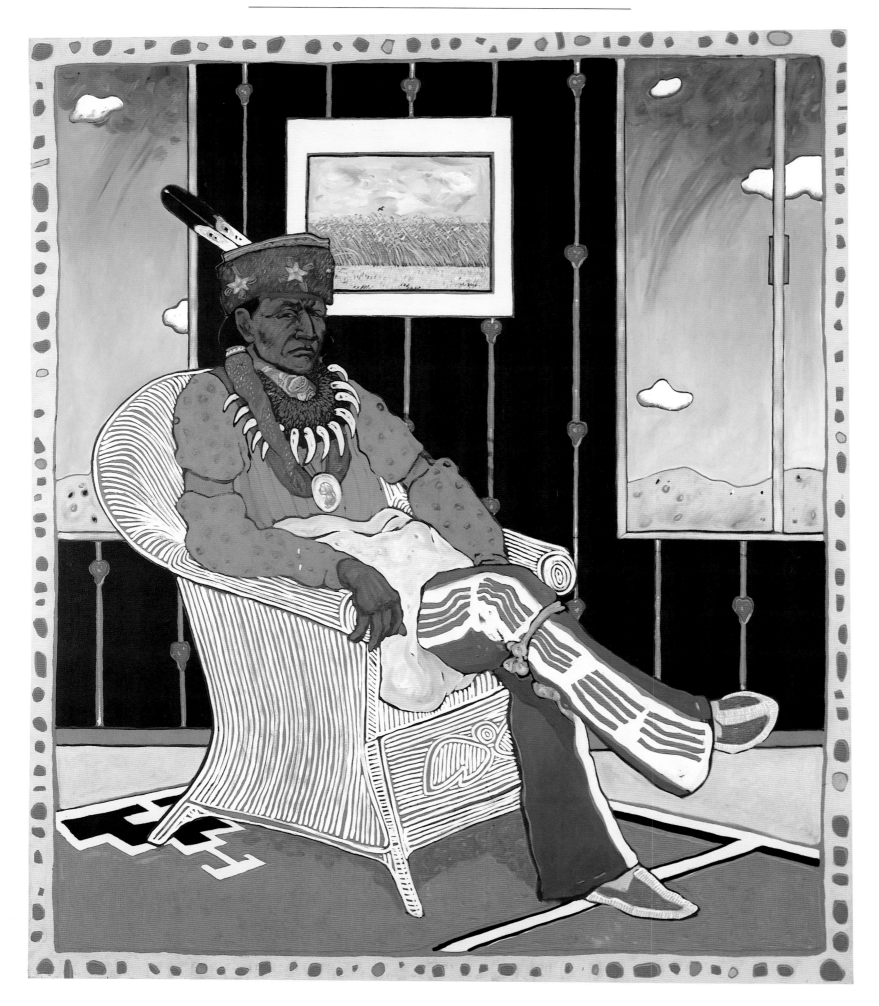

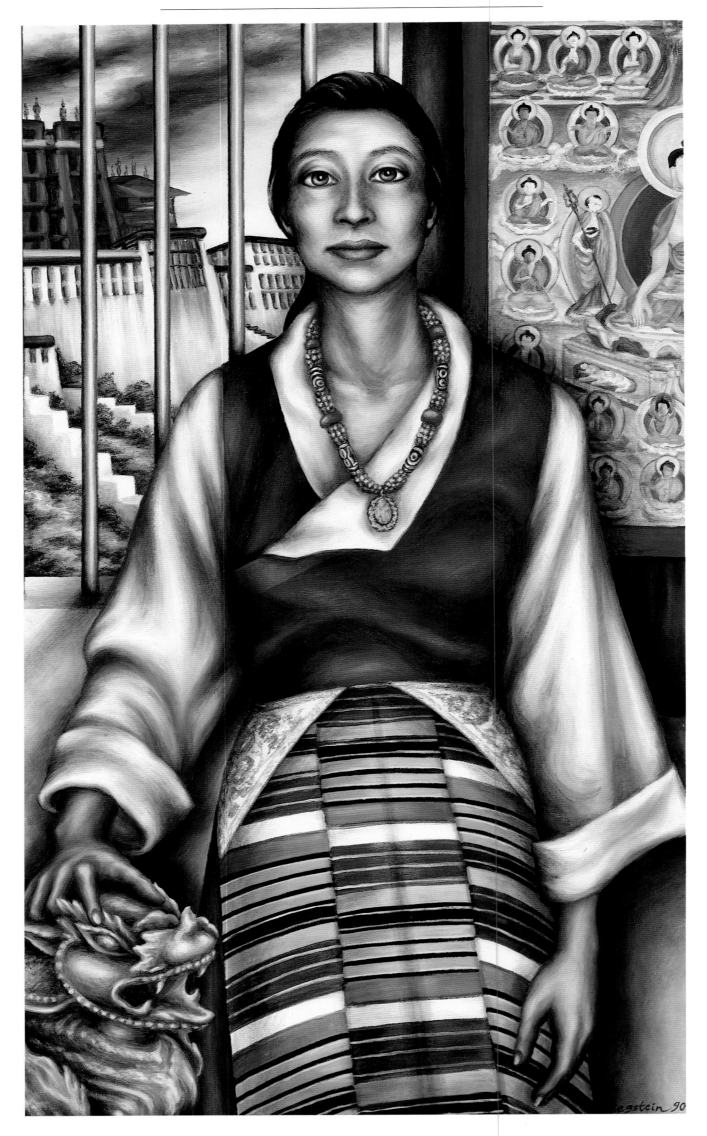

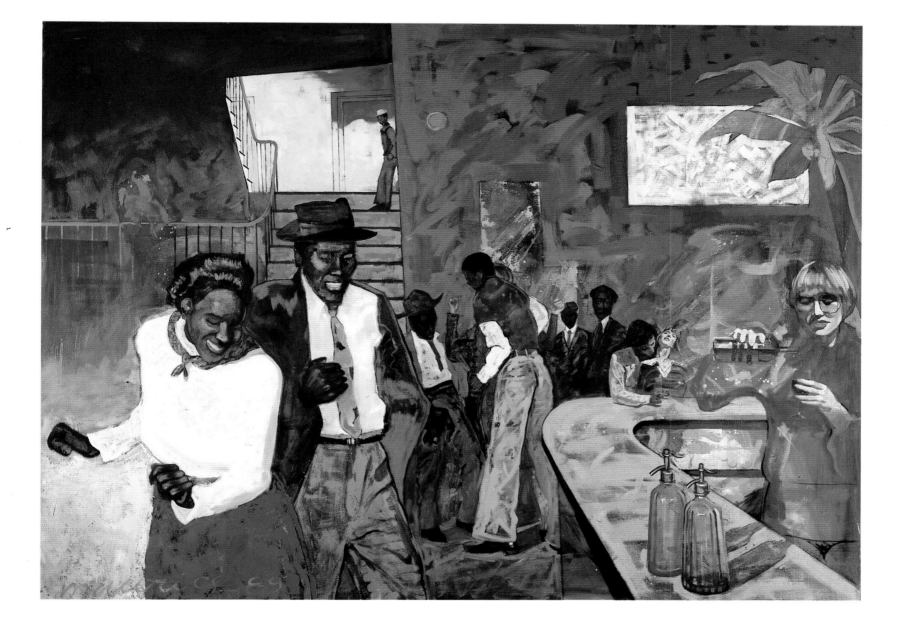

Left:
Zara Kriegstein (1952-)
Winds of Lhasa
1990, acrylic on canvas, 54 × 32 in.
Collection of Paljor and Tzering Thondup
Photo courtesy of the Turner Carroll Gallery, Santa Fe, NM

Maurice Burns (1937-)
All Night Long, II
1990, oil on canvas, 56 × 76 in.
Collection of Kathleen Peters

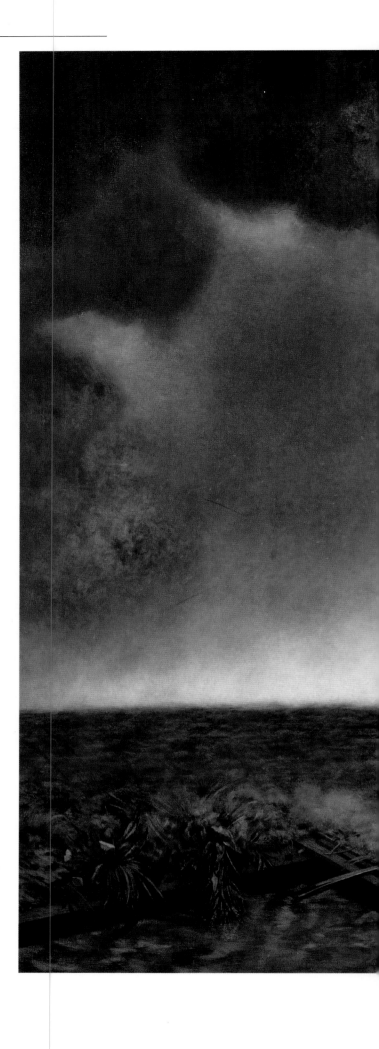

MARK SPENCER (1949-   )
Emergency
1990, oil on canvas, 72 × 96 in.
Collection of Marty and Laya Bloom, TX

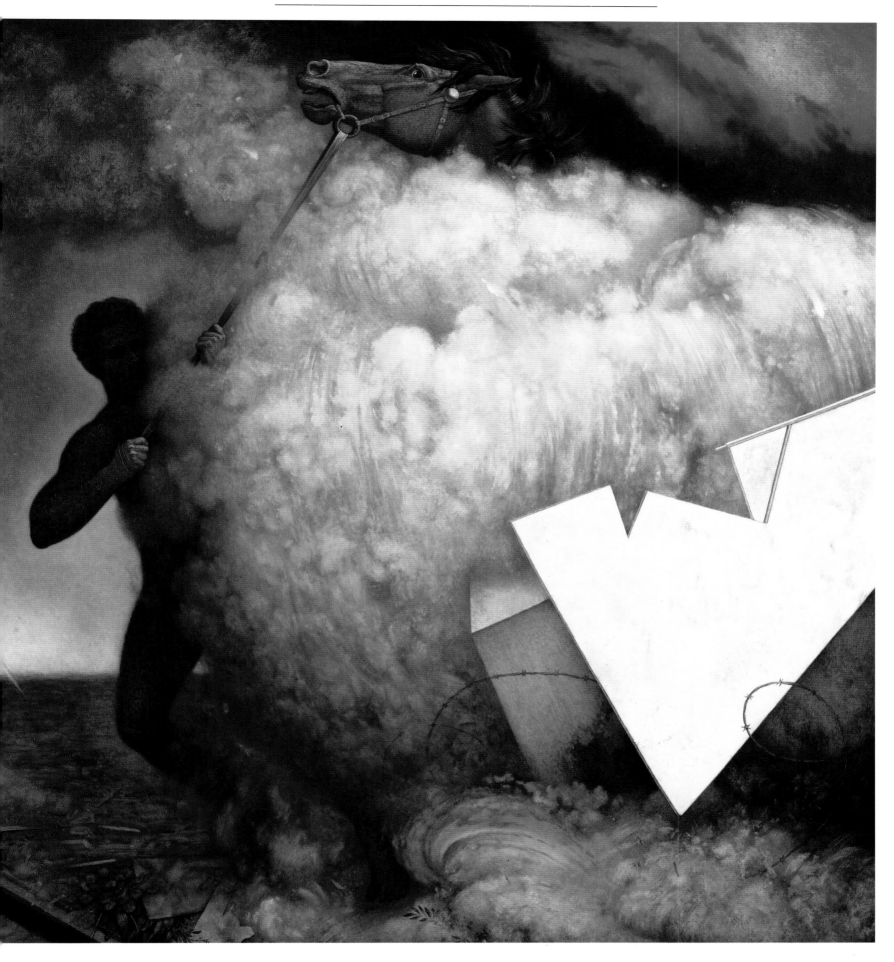

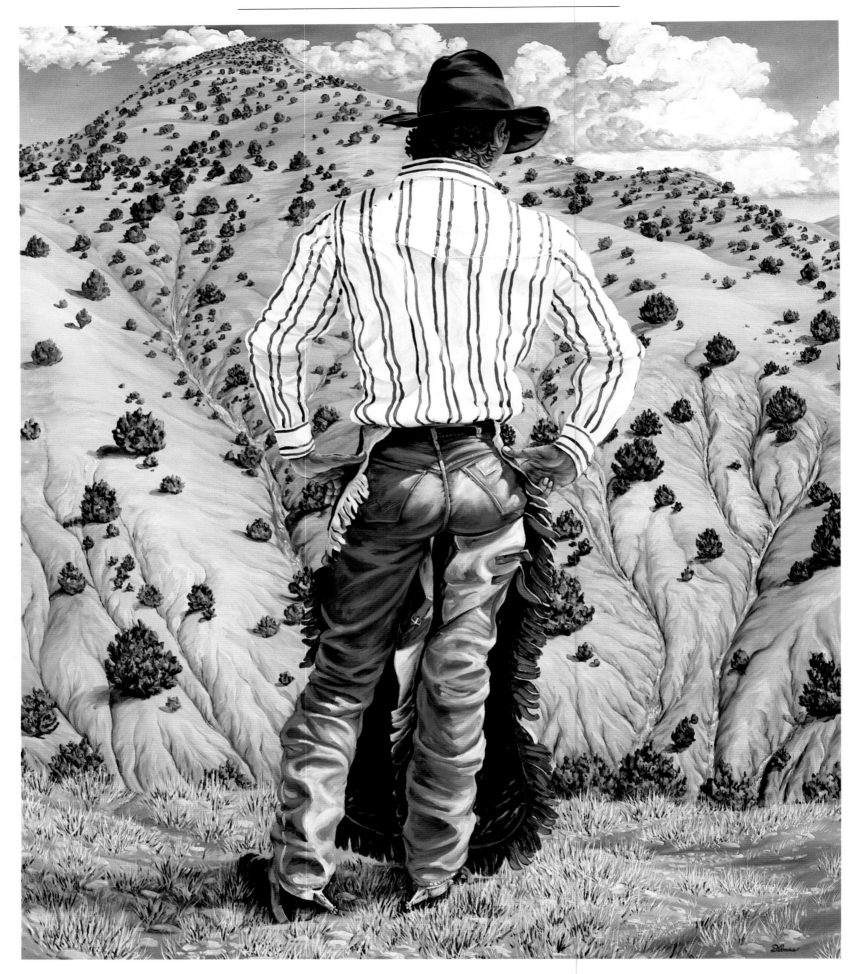

DELMAS HOWE (1935-   )
Apollo's Half Acre
1991, oil on canvas, 68 × 59 in.
Photo courtesy of Copeland-Rutherford Fine Arts, Ltd.,
    Santa Fe, NM

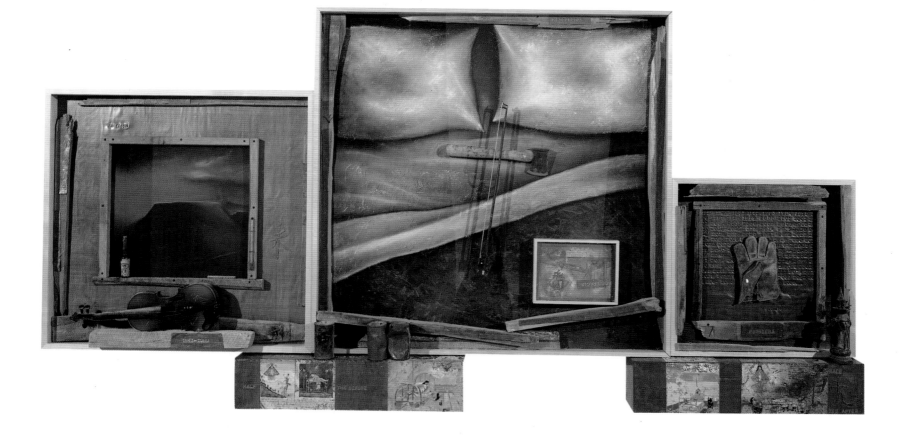

TERRY ALLEN (1943-)
Mascaradas en Busca de Gracia
1989, mixed media, overall height – 55⅞ in.,
    overall width – 111 in., overall depth – 5¾ in.
Museum League Purchase Fund
Dallas Museum of Art, TX

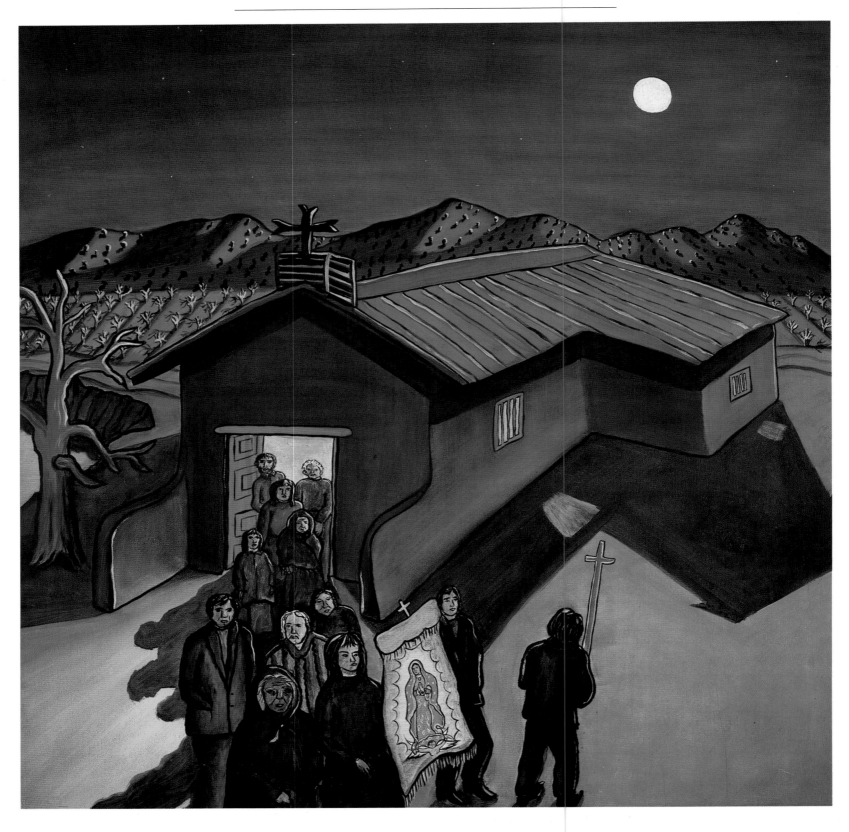

Bernadette Vigil (1955-)
La Procesión de la Virgen de Guadalupe
1991, oil on canvas, 30 × 30 in.
Courtesy of the Owings Dewey Fine Art Gallery, Santa Fe, NM

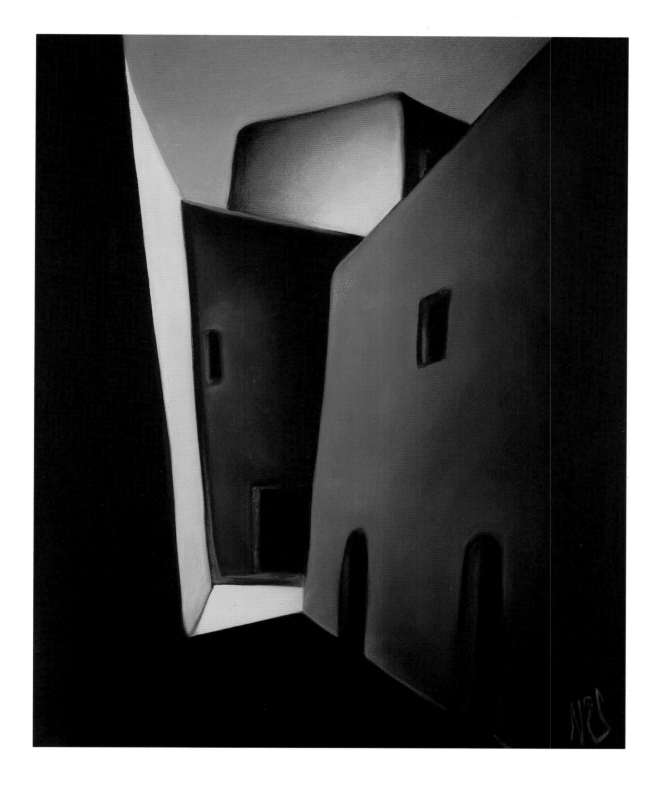

Margaret Nes (1950-   )
Passageway
1990, pastel on paper, 23¼ × 19 in.
Collection of John Kronstadt and Helen Bendix
Photo courtesy of the Edith Lambert Gallery, Santa Fe, NM

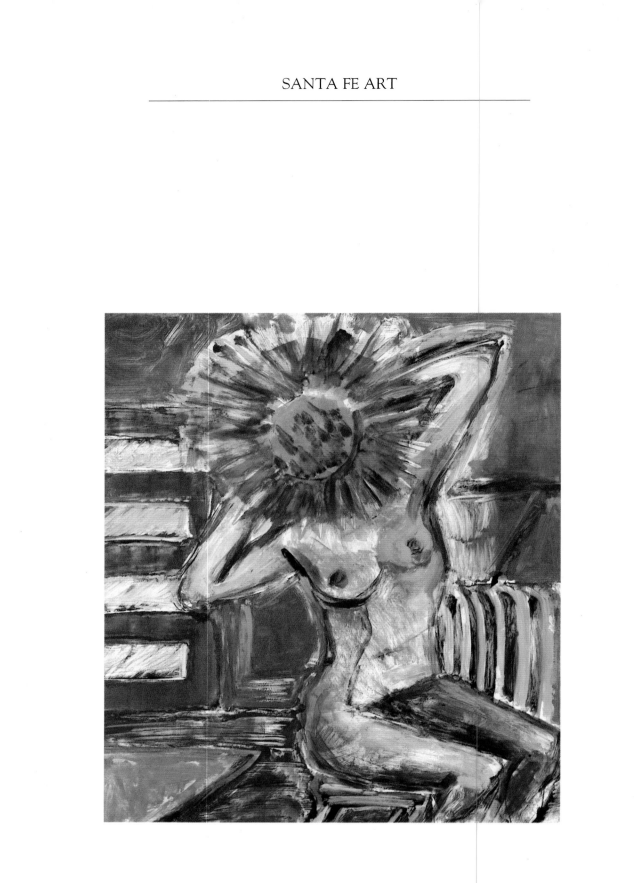

Darren Vigil Gray – Jicarilla Apache (1959-)
Blue Moon Light Sungirl # 1
c. 1991, monotype print, 36 × 30 in.
Permanent collection of the Institute of American Indian Arts
  Museum, Santa Fe, NM
Photo by Larry Phillips

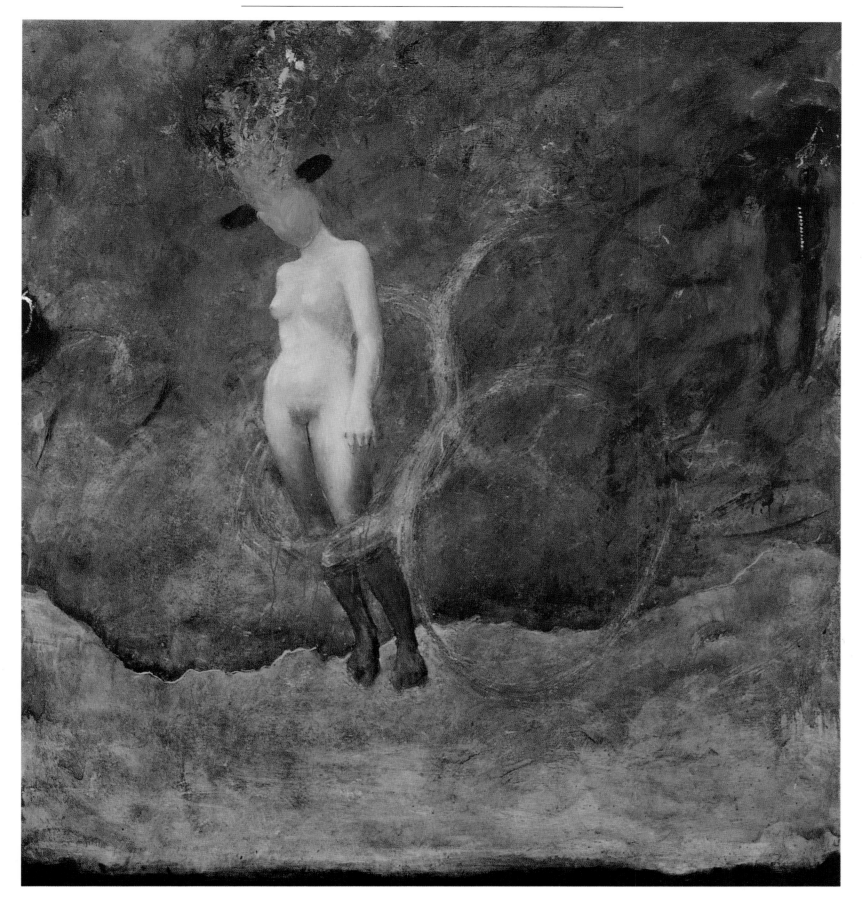

Kathleen Morris (1946-   )
Dream Circles
1989, oil on linen, 72 × 66 in.
Private Collection
Photo courtesy of the Artist

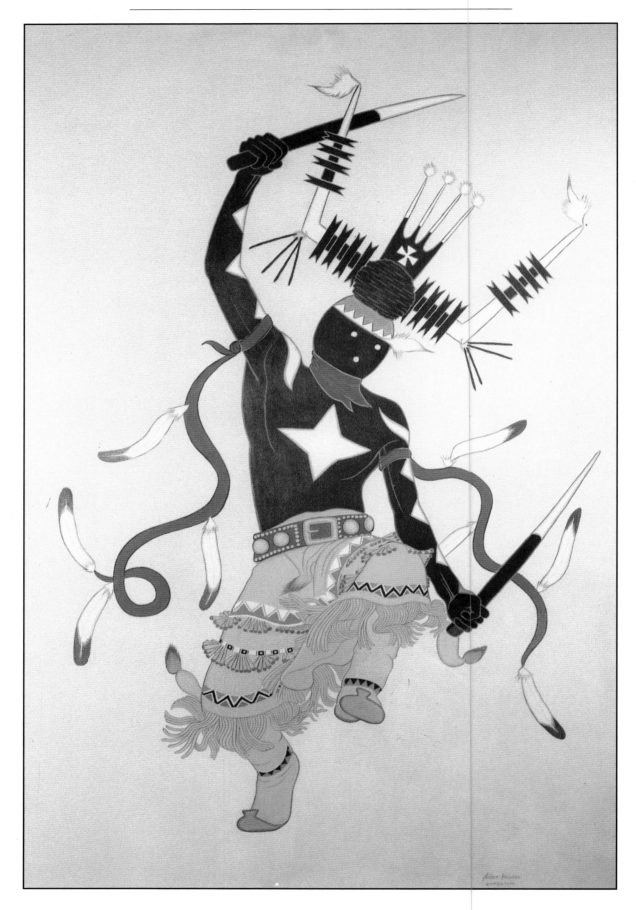

ALLAN HOUSER – CHIRICAHUA APACHE (1915-   )
Crown Dancer
c. 1954, casein on masonite, 65 × 46 in.
Permanent collection of the Institute of American Indian Arts
  Museum, Santa Fe, NM
Photo by Larry Phillips

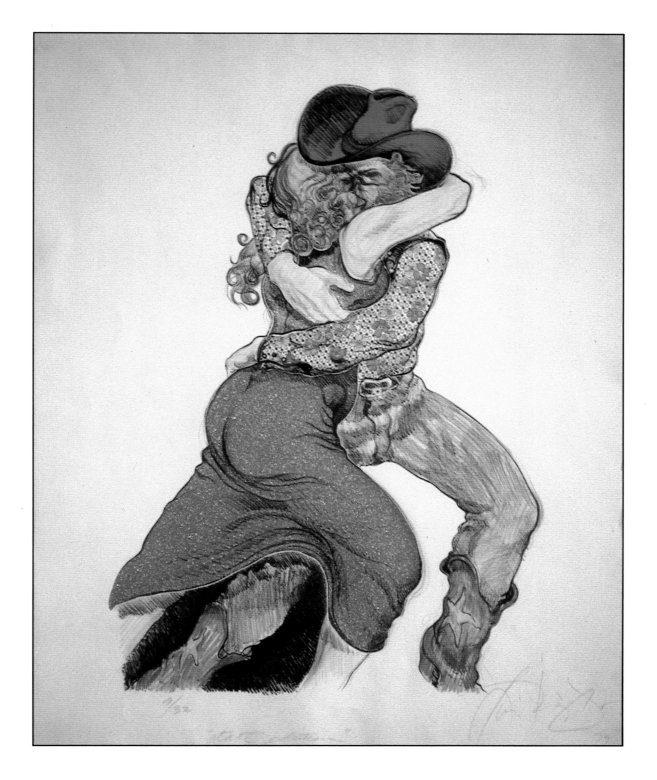

Luis Jimenez (1942-   )
Dancers
1979, litho/collage, 27¼ × 22½ in.
Courtesy of the LewAllen Gallery, Santa Fe, NM

ELIAS RIVERA (1937-)
Under the Portal
1991, oil on canvas, 66 × 108 in.
New Mexico State Capitol Building
Photo courtesy of the Munson Gallery, Santa Fe, NM

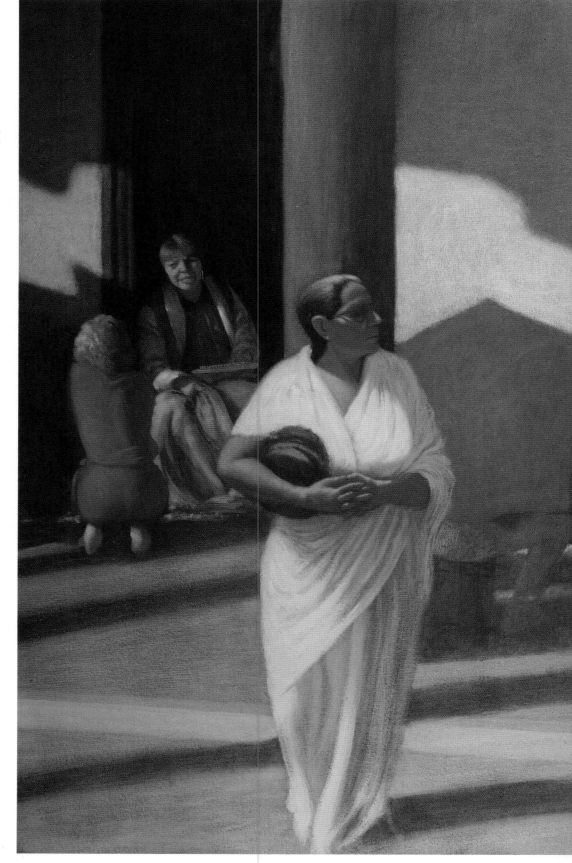

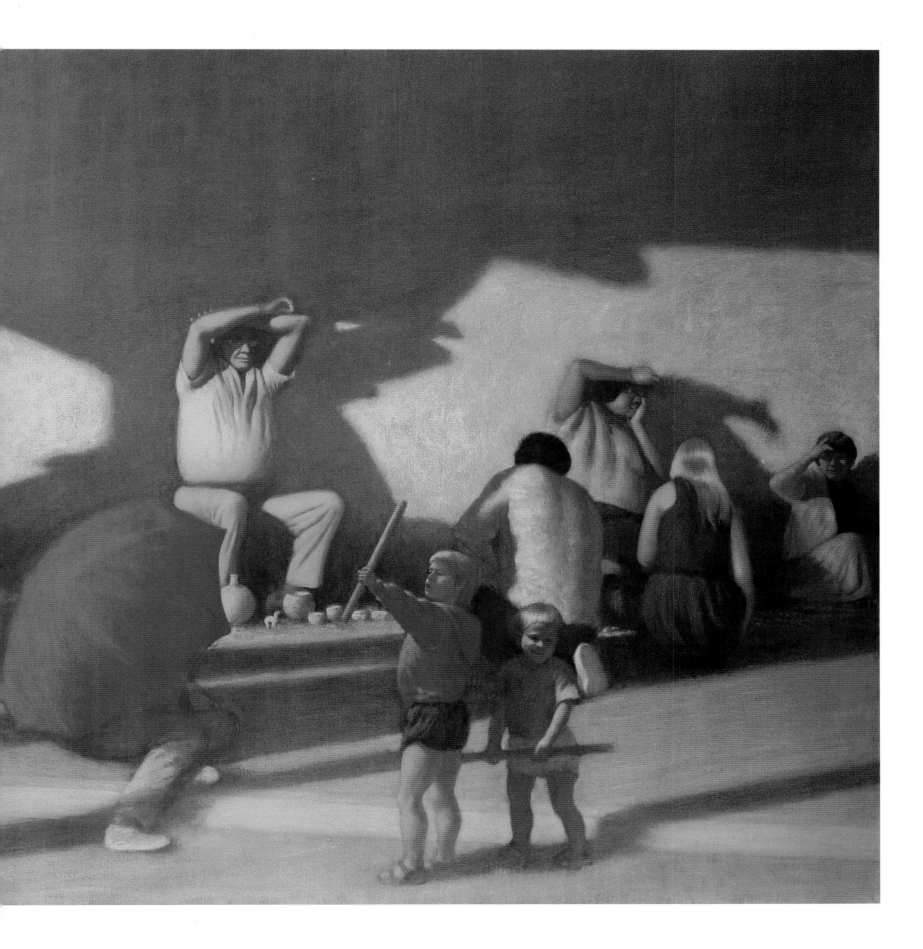

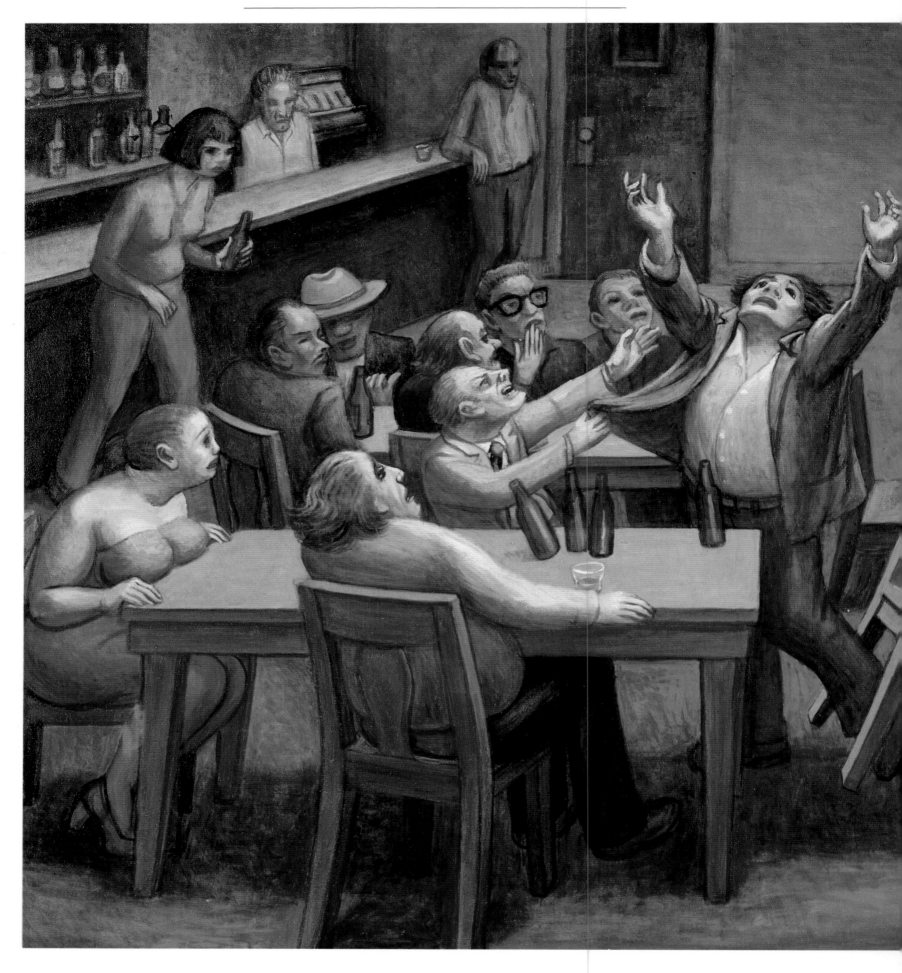

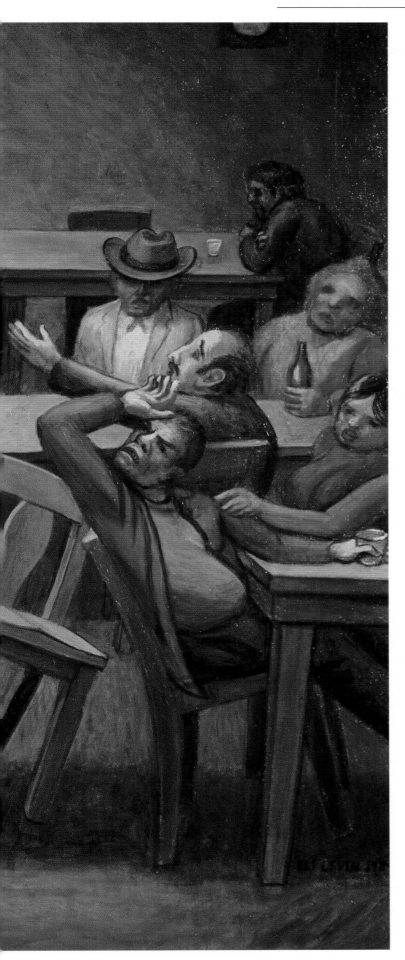

ELI LEVIN (1938-   )
Revelation
1985, oil on canvas, 36 × 48 in.
Photo courtesy of the Cline Fine Art Gallery, Santa Fe, NM

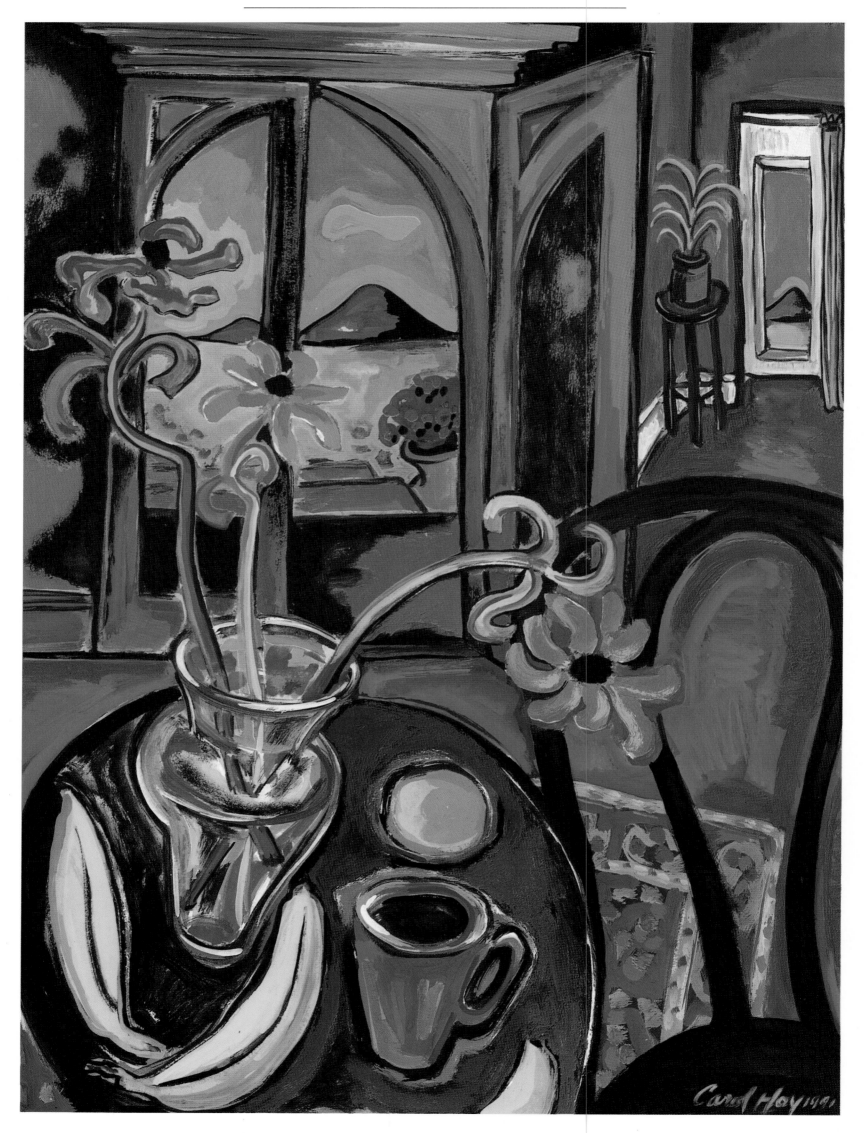

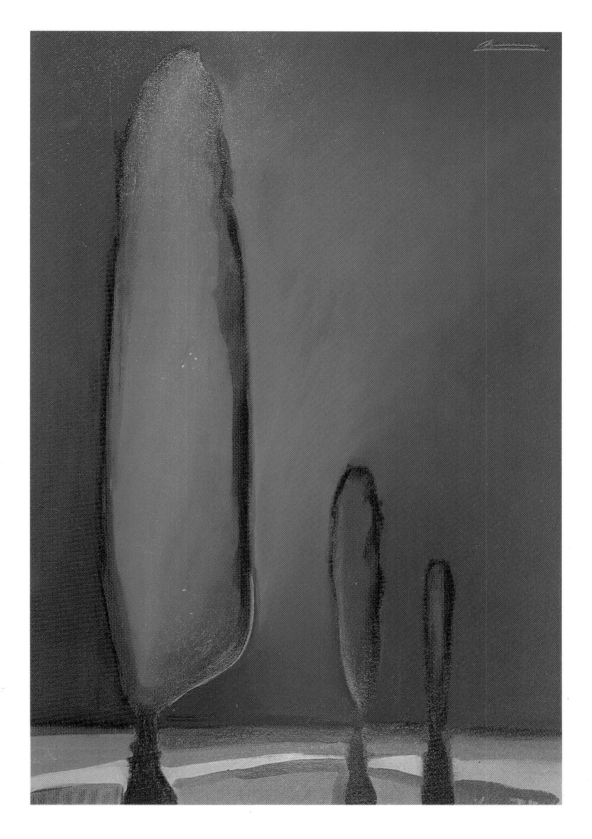

Left:
CAROL HOY (1948-)
Interior with Bananas and Anemones
1991, casein on paper, 30 × 22 in.
Collection of Dr. and Mrs. Rob Porter
Photo courtesy of the Edith Lambert Gallery, Santa Fe, NM

MATEO ROMERO – PUEBLO (1966-)
Red Poplars in Blue Sky
1992, oil on canvas, 60 × 40 in.
Photo courtesy of Copeland-Rutherford Fine Arts, Ltd.,
  Santa Fe, NM

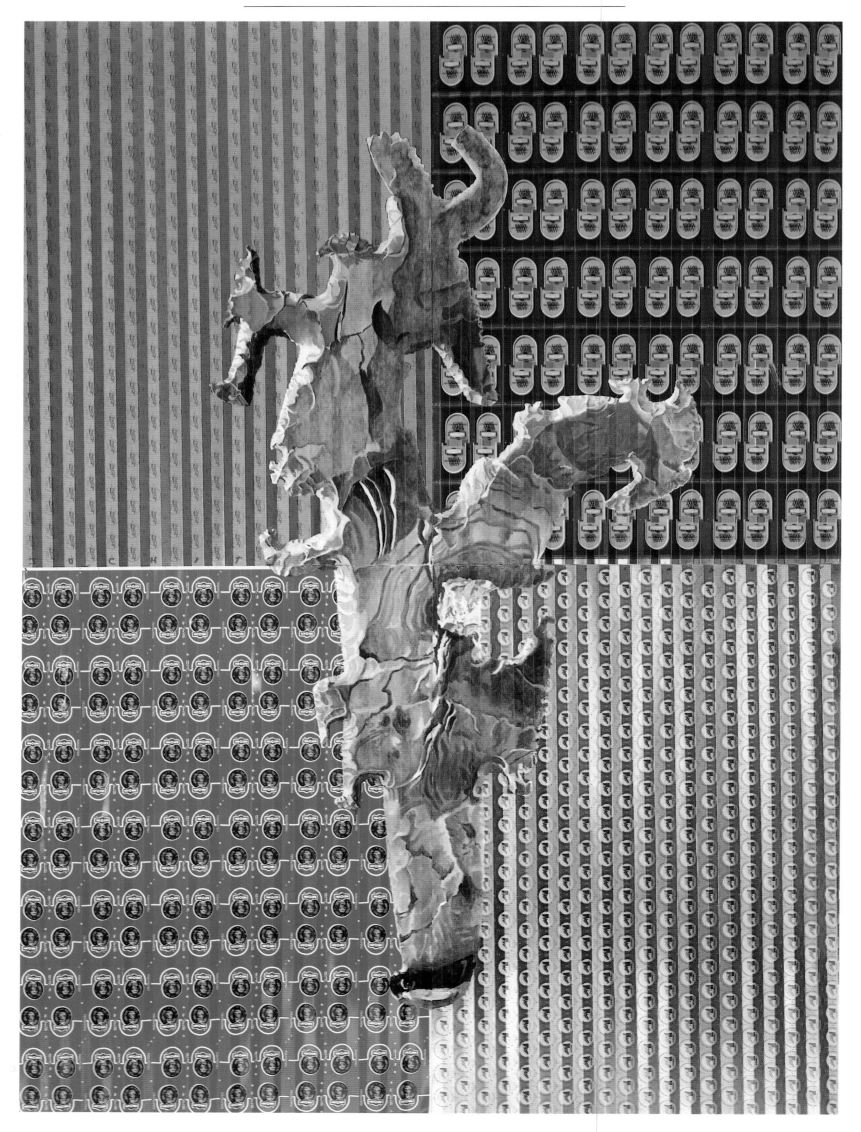

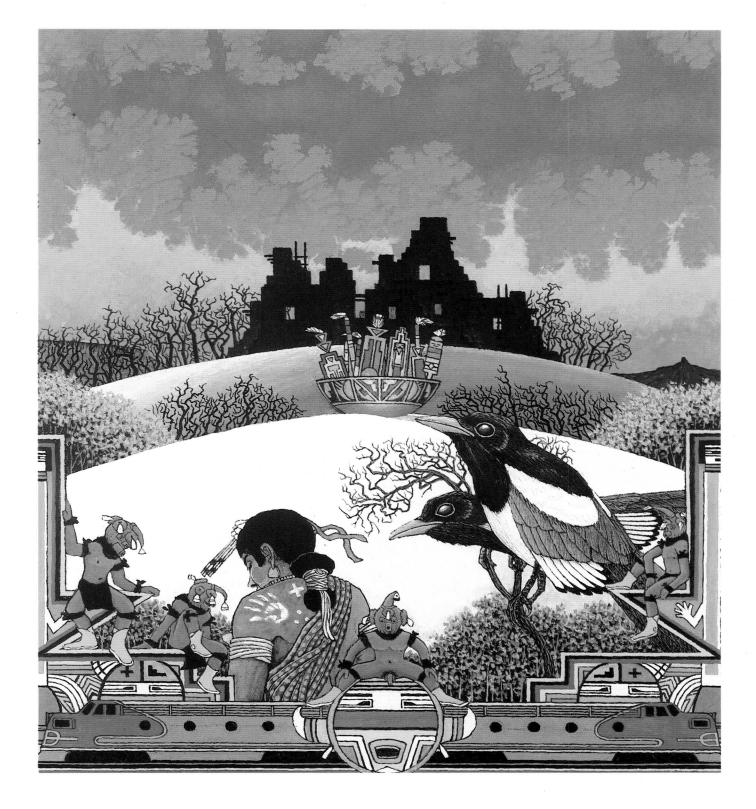

Left:
Ron Cooper (1943-)
Ceremonial Obsidian Hacha
1990, oil on lithographed tin panels, 70 × 51½ in.
Collection of Dennis Hopper, Venice, CA/Taos, NM
Photo by Paul O'Connor

Douglas Johnson (1946-)
Magpies
n.d., casein on paper, 8 × 7⅛ in.
Photo courtesy of the Gerald Peters Gallery, Santa Fe, NM

LIST OF COLOR PLATES

Picture Credits
All pictures were provided by the credited institution or individuals, except the following:
Ernest Blumenschein House: 9(top), 11(top).
Kit Carson Historic Museums, Taos, NM: 6
Walter Chappell: 13(bottom left).
Lisa Law: 7(top, bottom), 9(bottom right), 10, 11(bottom), 12, 14(all three), 17(all three), 18(both).
Museum of Fine Arts, Boston, MA: 15.

Museum of New Mexico, Photo Archives: 8(bottom), 11(center); Photo by T. Harmon Parkhurst: 7(center); Photo by Bert Phillips: 8(top).
University of Toledo, Ward M. Canaday Center: 13(bottom right).

Acknowledgements
Special thanks to Rena Rosequist at the Mission Gallery, Taos, for her invaluable assistance with this project, and to research assistants Sydney Davis and Tasha Roberts. Thanks also go to Rita Longabucco, the picture editor; Mike Rose, the designer; and Jean Martin, the editor.